"The key to living a life that leaves a legac[y] personal relationship with Jesus. This book presents a clear and simple process for using God's Word to form and build your lasting legacy."

—Lou Holtz, legendary football coach
and bestselling author of *Wins, Losses, and Lessons*

"Fundamentals. Simple. Basics. Commonsense. Practical. These words describe the recurring theme of Carl Newell's book, *Unlock Your Legacy*. As someone having lived a full, adventurous, and varied life, his message is boiled down to obvious truths that unfortunately, are not so obvious in today's Bible-rejecting culture. As he weaves in stories of real people to illustrate timeless Biblical principles, the message is clear—it is never too late to improve your legacy."

—Mike Huckabee, former Arkansas Governor,
author, and host of TBN's *The Huckabee Show*

"Knowing what you believe and why is vital to creating a legacy and living a life worth emulating. There is no greater legacy than glorifying God in how you live. I trust this book will encourage you to seek God's wisdom and understanding so that your legacy will be a life lived to honor and please the Lord."

—André Thornton, President and CEO, *ASW Global*
and former MLB player (1973–1987)

"*Unlock Your Legacy* addresses the issue of life's goals, even as we mature and have realized some of those goals. The premise of leaving a legacy may or may not resonate, but surely when looking back at our life, one might wonder what he or she could have done differently to make the world a better place. Newell provides a path that will get you thinking about your legacy and may even motivate you to actively pursue it, no matter your age."

—Dr. Darlene M. Iskra, PhD, Commander, U.S. Navy (Retired)
author of *Women in the United States Armed Forces: A Guide to the Issues*

"I have known Carl Newell for many years and once served as his pastor. His book touches a nerve that should hit everyone either today or tomorrow—the importance of your life's legacy. Everyone leaves a legacy; the question is just whether or not that legacy is worth leaving. Many nuggets of wisdom in this book may be used as "smooth stones" to fight the giants you will face in life. This book can help you live the kind of life you were made for by the God who created each of us. I know you will enjoy this work."

—Dr. James Merritt, PhD, Lead Pastor of Cross Pointe Church, Duluth, GA and past President of The Southern Baptist Convention

"This book is right on target spiritually; I especially like Chapter Four. I believe *Unlock Your Legacy* will be a blessing to everyone who reads it."

—Bobby Richardson, former MLB player, New York Yankees (1955–1966)

"Personal faith in Christ is the driving force of a meaningful legacy. This book provides insights and encouragement for creating a legacy of blessings to others."

—Rev. Andy Webb, Pastor, Mooresville (NC) ARP Church

"As one who has recently started a family and a ministry, leaving a legacy has become more important to me than ever. Carl lays out clear obstacles the Devil loves to use to distract us from focusing on our legacy. Chapter Four gives me the basic fundamentals of leaving a legacy through my family of origin, and my family of choice. So, if I get side-tracked, I can get back to the basics by using the simple illustration of putting my socks and shoes on correctly. Simple definitions, simple instructions."

—Jay Dan Gumm, Executive Director of *Forgiven Felons*, www.forgivenfelons.org

Unlock Your Legacy

Keys to a Life Worth Emulating

J. Carl Newell

1 THESS. 5:18

Unlock Your Legacy

Trilogy Christian Publishers A Wholly Owned Subsidiary of Trinity Broadcasting Network

2442 Michelle Drive Tustin, CA 92780

Manufactured in the United States of America

10 9 8 7 6 5 4 3 2 1

Library of Congress Cataloging-in-Publication Data is available.

ISBN: 978-1-64773-476-3

E-ISBN: 978-1-64773-477-0

To Martha
My best friend
My consistent compass
My wife

The spark from one fire lights another fire,
and there is a wind that plows down the path of history.
The spark that we send down the wind will ignite later generations.
It will not die.

John W. Gardner

Introduction

I've lived a long time and was actually paying attention and making astute observations part of the time!

One sad observation is that many obviously intelligent people are drifting aimlessly on life's stagnant *Sea of Regret* due to a reluctance to engage in the hard work of thinking and planning necessary for an impactful life.

Our meandering ways may lead us to unwittingly adopt the go-with-the-flow approach to life described in *Memoirs of a Geisha*, Arthur Golden's best-selling novel:

> *We lead our lives like water flowing down a hill, going more or less in one direction until we splash into something that forces us to find a new course.*

We all want to leave our mark on this world—to depart from it feeling assured that our life mattered. And that's why creating your legacy is important! Legacy is about focusing on things that will endure; it's about putting your personal stamp on the future of others...it's about teaching by example and passing on things of lasting value to those who will live on after us.

Your legacy is not shaped and defined at the end of the road but by every day's decisions. It is defined by the moments shared, the actions taken, and even by the responses made to mistakes and bad decisions. No matter how far down the road of life you've traveled, it's not too late to work on ending it well!

As age begins to catch up with you—as it surely will—your willingness to be adventurous and make life changes may wane. If so, get a grip and affirm that it's never too late to modify the aimlessness or misdirection in your life and seek ways to make meaningful progress toward creating a worthwhile legacy.

When the 80-year-old Roman statesman Cato surprised his friends by choosing to begin the study of Greek, they reacted predictably. In response to their queries as to how he could begin such a lengthy and demanding task at his age, Cato is said to have responded, "This is the youngest age I have left."

Much of life's disappointment and discouragement results from fear...fear of failure and apprehension of an uncertain future coupled with anxiety about what *they* will think. These are weapons used by the Devil to thwart progress toward creating your desired legacy.

More than 3000 years ago, a teenaged shepherd boy garnered his courage to face-off one-on-one with a massive giant named Goliath. You know the story...David was rock solid in his belief that it was God's will for him to go up against seemingly insurmountable odds. The strength of his belief plus *one smooth stone* led to victory.

Today, Satan will place giant-like obstacles in your path. You will find nuggets of truth—*smooth stones*—sprinkled throughout this book that God can use to encourage you to engage and be victorious. For example:

A Smooth Stone
When the time of need arrives,
the time for preparation has passed.

Through the years I've read at least portions of many books written by well-meaning writers who have a love affair with words but a hate relationship with brevity. Books with so many pages cluttered with so many words that readers like me become glassy-eyed and lay them aside early on—their message never communicated and forever lost.

My desire for *Unlock Your Legacy* is that it be a down to earth, easy to read book with common-sense ideas and suggestions to help folks move from where they are to where they want to be. Fundamentally, it's to help you figure out where you are in life, where you want to be, and stimulate you to self-motivation to move in the necessary direction.

I am not a psychologist, theologian, or mystic. I'm just a simple guy who has traveled many roads in life and wants to help you avoid, eliminate and remove as many obstacles as possible *before* you become irreparably scarred. If you're already wounded by careening off the sharp edges of life, my desire is to help you pick yourself up, dust off any clinging crud, and assure you that God wants to lead you to a better life.

The purpose of this book is to provoke your thinking to choose a life you will enjoy while making significant progress toward creating the meaningful legacy you want to leave behind...a legacy that blesses many people you will never know.

Finally, in the interest of transparency I confess that everything written in this book was heavily influenced by these personal beliefs:

1. The Bible is the inspired Word of God and is without error.
2. Life begins at conception and never ends.
3. Every person is a two-in-one—an infinite *spiritual* being cleverly but temporarily encapsulated in a *human* body.

J. Carl Newell
Loganville, Georgia

Table of Contents

Chapter 1
Beginnings

In the beginning, God created the heavens and the earth.

Time. The undefinable continuous progress of existence and events occurring in irreversible succession from the past through the present and into the future.

At the beginning of the beginning, time did not exist. Nothing but a universal void filled with darkness existed. Nothing else. Nothing. So much nothing that there was no "there" there.

Then, God spoke the heavens and earth into existence and for good measure, created light to be the equal opposite of darkness. However, the ultimate source of light necessary to create and sustain the measurable parameters known as time—segmented into day and night—did not yet exist.

The first second of the first minute of the first hour of measurable time was initiated by a single spark.[1] One spark created the prime element of our cosmos by igniting a flaming ball of hydrogen and helium. The result was a star having a diameter of 864,000 miles and a surface temperature of 10,000 degrees Fahrenheit, an eternal flame that never burns up and never burns out. This star—our sun—was strategically placed at the most critically precise location in our solar system.[2]

Since nothing occurs outside universal laws, this amazing creative event must have an explanation. The Law of Cause and Effect dictates that the result of every action is a reaction or a consequence, i.e. an effect. Since the sun's explosion into existence was the effect of a spontaneous action, the next logical question becomes, "What—or Who—sparked the spark necessary to ignite the hydrogen and helium?"

A logical common-sense analysis concludes:

a. If an *effect* occurs, a *causer* must exist.

b. A causer creating a spark from nothing is a *creator*.

c. Therefore, the causer of the initial spark was a Creator.

The immutable truth of the Bible identifies the Creator setting off this magnificent chain of events. His name is Jesus. A succinct biographical note states:

> In the beginning was the Word, and the Word was with God, and the Word was God. He was in the beginning with God. All things were made through Him and without Him nothing was made that was made.

John 1:1-3

Creator Jesus did not stop with the creation of the sun! He immediately began to populate the universe with galaxies of planets, moons, and an innumerable array of stars. The sun is special to us but is just one of billions of stars scattered across the Milky Way galaxy. Though our sun is 109 thousand times the size of earth, it appears small because it is 93 million miles away! To put it in perspective, if the sun were the size of a typical front door, the earth would be the size of a nickel.[2]

God saved His most amazing creation for last![3] This 22-word biblical description of His creation of mankind forms perhaps the single most important sentence ever written or spoken:

> So God created man in His own image; in the image of God, He created him; male and female He created them.

Step-by-step, the final touches to implement His creative plan were added when an environmentally friendly home was provided for these first human beings. Actually, it was far more than adequate; it was an exquisitely beautiful garden developed eastward in Eden!

The first dawn in the inhabited Garden of Eden must have been inexplicably splendid in its beauty...but you were not there to enjoy it.

Like clockwork throughout many millennia, beautiful sunrises and sunsets have been visible from earth but you did not enjoy their magnificence.

You did not enjoy these phenomena because there was no you!

The Beginning of You

Not so very long ago, another incredibly creative event occurred to alter the course of history. *You* were conceived[4] and after an arduous nine months, made a screaming entry into the world. Interestingly, you were born unique... just like everyone else!

Thousands of years before your birth, a son was born to a young Jewish girl. This boy became a shepherd and as a young man, climbed the ladder of success to become the revered King David of Israel.

As king, David reflected upon the marvelous way in which the unchanging God created him and laid out a plan for his life:[5]

> Oh yes, you shaped me first inside, then out;
>   you formed me in my mother's womb.
> I thank you, High God—you're breathtaking!
>   Body and soul, I am marvelously made!
>   I worship in adoration—what a creation!
> You know me inside and out,
>   you know every bone in my body;
> You know exactly how I was made, bit by bit,
>   how I was sculpted from nothing into something.
> Like an open book, you watched me grow from conception
> to birth;
>   all the stages of my life were spread out before you,
> The days of my life all prepared
>   before I'd even lived one day.

Not unlike David, you were custom made by God. You are a one-of-a-kind

11

person of immeasurable value and unimaginable worth, so special that Jesus prayed for you centuries before your birth. Referring to those who had already believed in Him as Messiah and for future generations, Jesus prayed: "I do not pray for these alone, but also *for those who will believe* in Me through their word" (John 17:20, emphasis added).

Since God went to the trouble of uniquely creating you and Jesus prayed specifically for you, it is important to remember that you were created for a purpose. The Bible clearly states that each of us has a specific role in God's master plan:

> "For we are His workmanship, created in Christ Jesus for good works, which God prepared beforehand that we should walk in them" (Ephesians 4:10).

> "For I know the plans I have for you," says the LORD. "They are plans for good and not for disaster, to give you a future and a hope" (Jeremiah 29:11, NLT).

Your current assignment is to accept responsibility for identifying your life's purpose and then living it into reality. Every decision you make moves you closer to—or further from—accomplishing your purpose.

As we seek God's direction, we may find He has a detour in mind for us. He will guide us—if we allow Him—down paths He chooses for our success. We must determine where we are, decide where we want to be in the future and chart a course of action. The following chapters provide insight on ways to identify and revise the areas of your life needing improvement.

Twenty years from now, you will arrive. The question is, "Where?" The purpose of this book is to provoke your thinking to choose a future you will appreciate and enjoy by living a life worth emulating.

A Smooth Stone
Some futures are better than others. Choose wisely!

Chapter Notes

1. Even if we knew—and no one does—the technique God used in creating the sun, we are woefully inadequate to understand the process. God's wonderful gift of imagination was used to posit a logical hypothesis using a spark to illustrate this mysterious, magnificent event.

2. The sun is a star, a hot ball of glowing gases at the heart of our solar system. Without the sun's intense energy and heat, there would be no life on Earth. Scientists estimate the temperature at the sun's surface is 10,000 degrees Fahrenheit; at its core, the temperature is about 27 million degrees Fahrenheit. Equally impressive is the enormity of the sun's relative size to planet earth. Source: www.nasa.gov/sun

3. Lest the dogmatic assertions of ego-driven pseudo-intellectuals confuse your thinking, remember these facts outlined in Genesis 1:27-28:
    a. God created just two genders—male and female.
    b. The marriage relationship ordained by God consists of one man and one woman.

4. Everyone seems to agree that *something* is formed at conception. One vital question the Pro-Choice movement has not adequately answered to my satisfaction is, "If that *something* is not a human being, what is it?" A more critical question is, "At which point on the nine-month gestation timeline does the non-specific *something* become a human being worthy of being allowed to be born?"

5. Psalm 139:13-16, *The Message* (MSG), Copyright © 1993, 2002, 2018 by Eugene H. Peterson.

Chapter 2
The Wonder of You

I will praise You, for I am fearfully and wonderfully made.
Marvelous are Your works, and that my soul knows very well.
—Psalm 139:14

In awe of the Creator's magnificent work in and around him, the psalmist left a template we can follow in seeking to live a life worth emulating:

1. Acknowledge that you were created as an extraordinarily unique person gifted with specific abilities.
2. Praise Him early and often. Make praising Him a continuous habit. He is certainly worthy of your gratefulness and praise!

Approximately one hundred years ago, Dr. Frank Crane[1] wrote an interesting essay titled *The Man Inside*. This brief essay effectively describes the marvelous effects of our Creator's constant and consistent attention to detail. Although we rarely consider the perpetual miracles occurring within our body, He keeps them in sync and working for us 24 hours a day, every day of the year.

> The smartest man in the world is the Man Inside. By the Man Inside, I mean that Other Man within each one of us that does most of the things we give ourselves credit for doing. You may refer to him as Nature or the Subconscious Self or think of him merely as Force or a Natural Law, or if you are religiously inclined, you may use the term God.

> I say he is the smartest man in the world. I know he is infinitely cleverer and more resourceful than I am or than any other man is that I ever heard of. When I cut my finger, it is he that calls up the little phagocytes to come and kill the septic germs that might get into the wound and cause blood poisoning. It is he that coagulates the blood, stops the gash, and weaves the new skin.

15

I could not do that. I do not even know how he does it. He even does it for babies that know nothing at all; in fact, does it better for them than for me.

No living man knows enough to make toenails grow, but the Man Inside thinks nothing of growing nails and teeth and thousands of hairs all over my body; long hairs on my head and little fuzzy ones over the rest of the surface of the skin.

When I practice on the piano, I am simply getting the business of piano playing over from my conscious mind to my subconscious mind. In other words, I am handing the business over to the Man Inside.

Most of our happiness, as well as our struggles and misery, come from this Man Inside. If we train him in ways of contentment, adjustment, and decision, he will go ahead of us like a well-trained servant and do for us easily most of the difficult tasks we have to perform.

Your Marvelous Mind

In the *really* early days of medical practice, the ancient Greek physician Hippocrates (460 BC–375 BC), often called the Father of Medicine, observed, "I am of the opinion that the brain exercises the greatest power in the man." He believed that the totality of human power and potential is neatly tucked away within a three-pound mushroom of gray and white tissue called the brain.

Most of us spend little to no time thinking about our brains. We may think of it in terms of a Master Control Center maintaining a complex operating system necessary to continue living. Or we may see our brain as simply the place where our *mind* resides.

The brain is actually a super-efficient manager/supervisor of all our bodily needs and functions. While handling all the complex details, our brain lets us think that we feel with our fingers, taste with our tongue, and hear with our ears. In reality, all these sensations occur inside the brain—the fingers, tongue, and ears are simply gatherers of information.

Our Creator designed the brain to handle millions of disparate tasks continuously. From mundane tasks—like telling us when we're hungry—to incredibly critical tasks like initiating complex healing and life-saving processes when we are hurt or traumatized.

While every human being is a unique creation, each has been equipped with the same capability to build a meaningful, God-honoring life. The two greatest available sources of power for defining and achieving success are the conscious mind and the subconscious mind.

The Power of the Conscious Mind

The conscious mind is controlled by your thoughts and serves as the Intelligence Center that directs your behavior. Whenever you have a direct experience such as a conversation with a friend, stepping on a snake, or becoming aware of a serious problem, stimuli from the experience enters your nervous system through one of the five primary senses. The experience is instantly transmitted to your conscious mind, you think about it and respond with behavior.

Man's understanding of the complexity and power of the brain and the mind it contains is extremely limited. Many scientists and psychologists believe the conscious mind exercises a relatively small degree of control over our mental life. They generally agree that the conscious mind:

» Is objective. It can reason and rationalize.
» Provides the faculty of knowing one's own thoughts.
» Controls voluntary functions and motions.
» Discriminates between right and wrong, wise and foolish.
» Decides to plan and prepare or to drift aimlessly through life.

A key function of the conscious mind is its focus on personal desires. As such, it is the primary input to the *subconscious* mind which scientists believe directs and controls most of our mental life.

The Power of the Subconscious Mind

The subconscious mind is a tireless manager of your body's vital functions and the brain's vast, immeasurable database of information and experiences. Many years ago, Robert Collier[2] tauntingly described the brilliant work of the subconscious mind:

> Can you tell me how much water, how much salt, how much of each different element there should be in your blood to maintain its proper specific gravity if you are leading an ordinary sedentary life? How much and how quickly these proportions must be changed if you play a fast game of tennis, or run for your car, or chop wood, or indulge in any other violent exercise?
>
> Do you know how much water you should drink to neutralize the excess salt in salt fish? Do you know how much water, how much salt, how much of each different element in your food should be absorbed into your blood each day to maintain perfect health?
>
> No? Well, it need not worry you. Neither does anyone else. Not even the greatest physicists and chemists and mathematicians. But your subconscious mind knows.

Complementing its built-in intelligence, the subconscious mind subjectively processes informational input. It does not think or reason independently but simply obeys orders received from the conscious mind. The subconscious mind generates physical and/or emotional distress when you attempt to do something new, different, or inconsistent with your strong beliefs.

Every piece of information accepted by the conscious mind is delivered to the subconscious mind. The subconscious mind accepts every bit of data, information, and opinion as truth, even though some of it may not accurately reflect reality. *The strength of a specific belief apparently determines its relative priority within the subconscious.*

Since the subconscious accepts everything received from the conscious mind as absolute truth, Henry Ford[3] was spot on when he observed, "If you think you can do a thing or think you can't do a thing, you're right."

It's noteworthy to recognize that your *personal faith* in God provides the linkage necessary for the subconscious mind to form the bridge between your conscious mind and Infinite Intelligence, i.e., the mind of God.

The Brain's Database

Some awesome wonders of the universe pale into insignificance when compared to the complexity, capability, and storage capacity of the brain. Many scientists and physicians view the brain as a recording mechanism having an infinite storage capacity.

Consider this opinion of the renowned neurosurgeon, Dr. Ben S. Carson:[4]

> The organ system of the brain is one of incredible complexity and power. It can process millions of pieces of information per second. *It remembers everything a person has ever seen or heard.* For example, by placing special electrodes into the parts of the brain that control memory, you can stimulate recall in an 85 year–old so specific that he could quote verbatim a newspaper article read a half-century earlier. (Emphasis added).

Dr. Carson's insight corroborates a fascinating medical event reported at a 1950's meeting of the National Academy of Sciences. In his book *Psycho-Cybernetics*, Dr. Maxwell Maltz[5] referred to a presentation made by Dr. Wilder Penfield[6] describing the discovery of a recording capability located within a small area of the brain. Everything a person has ever experienced, observed, or learned is apparently faithfully recorded within this portion of the brain.

During an operation in which the patient was fully awake, Dr. Penfield reportedly touched a small area of the brain's cortex with a surgical instrument. The patient immediately exclaimed that she was "reliving" an incident from her childhood. Dr. Penfield later concluded that the brain performs three functions: recording, recalling, and reliving.

In addition to Drs. Carson, Maltz, and Penfield, other scientists believe that your wondrous brain has indelibly recorded every nuance of every experience of your life...every word, every scent, every feeling.

Jesus was obviously aware of the brain's amazing capabilities when He prophetically proclaimed to religious leaders in Jerusalem, "But I say to you that for *every idle word* men may speak, they will give account of it in the day of judgment" (Matthew 12:36, emphasis added).

A Spiritual Perspective

Religious leaders in Jesus' day made it their primary goal to belittle and discredit Him. When publicly asked, "Which is the foremost commandment of all?" Jesus responded:

> The first of all the commandments is: "Hear O Israel, the LORD our God, the LORD is one. And you shall love the LORD your God with all your heart, with all your soul, with all your mind, and with all your strength."
>
> Mark 12:28-29

To love the Lord "with all your mind" necessities an ability to synchronize the conscious and subconscious minds. Seeking to understand the plausibility and possibility of such an ability, many Christians look to this Scripture: "He makes my feet like the feet of deer, and sets me on my high places" (Psalm 18:33, *see also* Habakkuk 3:19).

They seek to adopt what is likely a reference to a *physical* deliverance to define the *spiritual* process God instituted for correlating our conscious and subconscious minds.

Exploring the same mystery, Glenn Clark[7] prayerfully sought spiritual insight and wrote this allegorical explanation of the psalmist's assertion:

> No animal has such perfect correlation of its front and rear feet as does the deer. While the male deer, or the hart, is a wonder of surefootedness, still more wonderful is the female, or the hind, which, while leading its young into hidden fastnesses, is the most perfect example of physical correlation that God has ever made.
>
> And this was the blinding revelation: *As the feet of the hind are to the mountains, so is the mind of man to the heights of life; and as the rear feet of the hind are to the front feet, so is the subconscious mind of man to the conscious mind.* And as the creature which has the most perfect correlation between its front and its rear feet is the surest to reach the mountaintop in safety, so the person who has the most perfect correlation between his conscious mind and his subconscious mind is the surest to reach the heights of life.
>
> Our lips speak the thoughts of our conscious mind, but only the heart speaks the thoughts of our subconscious mind. "As a man thinketh in his heart, so is he." "Out of the heart come the issues of life."
>
> And when the lips and the heart are in alignment, when they track together with the absolute certainty that the rear feet of the deer track with the front feet, then *nothing* is impossible, whether it be the climbing of mountains or the casting of mountains into the seas

Later in his book, Mr. Clark took an introspective look at himself:

> Where did my conscious and subconscious mind track together? This was one of the first questions to be answered.

21

How many things had I done with all my strength, with all my mind, and with all my heart, and with all my soul—in other words, with "all four feet?" Pitifully few, I had to confess to myself.

Striving to create our legacy by living a life worth following, we must likewise critically examine ourselves and take action to bring our conscious and subconscious minds into closer alignment.

Fortunately, our Creator equipped each of us with every tool and all the materials we will ever need to create and build a lasting legacy...a life worth emulating.

Chapter Notes

1. Dr. Frank Crane (1861–1928) was a Presbyterian Minister and author. This essay is included in his set of ten volumes titled *Four Minute Essays* published in 1919.

2. Robert Collier (1885–1950) was the author of *The Secret of the Ages,* copyright 1948.

3. Henry Ford (1863–1947) was an American industrialist and founder of the Ford Motor Company. He pioneered the development of the assembly line technique of mass production.

4. Dr. Benjamin S. Carson (b. 1951) was formerly Director of Pediatric Neurosurgery at the Johns Hopkins Children's Center. In 1987, he gained worldwide recognition as the principal surgeon in the 22–hour separation of the Binder Siamese twins from Germany. After his retirement, Dr. Carson served as the 17th United States Secretary of Housing and Urban Development. Source of quotation: *Parade Magazine,* December 7, 2003.

5. Dr. Maxwell Maltz (1899–1975) was an American cosmetic surgeon and author of *Psycho-Cybernetics.* His book presents a system of ideas and processes designed to help improve one's self-image.

6. Dr. Wilder G. Penfield (1891–1976) was one of Canada's foremost neurosurgeons and is best known for the discovery of a surgical treatment for epilepsy. He was the founder and first director of the world-famous Montreal Neurological Institute.

7. Glenn Clark (1882–1956) was a professor of literature and an athletic coach at Macalester College in Saint Paul, MN for thirty years. He was a deeply religious man and a great believer in prayer. In 1942, he resigned his position at the college to devote his life to helping others discover the integration of body, mind, and spirit in God. Information Source: *I Will Lift Up Mine Eyes*, Copyright 1937 by Harper & Brothers.

Chapter 3
Life — A Perspective

Life is lived forward but understood backward.
—Søren Kierkegaard[1]

Life is tough. It's even tougher when you're stupid![2]

Fortunately, stupidity—and ignorance— are manageable factors in life. We can acquire and apply knowledge and wisdom simply by paying attention as life unfolds around us and by listening to and learning from others whose lives are worth emulating.

The ancient Greek philosopher Aristotle[3] said, "First, know thyself; second, understand others and finally, learn of the world around you." I don't know whether Mr. A actually made the statement but am convinced he would agree with its wisdom. It just makes sense ... and yet, most academic curricula focus primarily on teaching *the world around you.*

Consider the time, energy, and other resources invested in the third Aristotelian category. Literally, years are spent learning math, science, geography, biology, linguistics, grammar, information technology, and debating whether there are two or two hundred genders.

Indeed, some courses, e.g. history, sociology, civics, and public speaking may fit into the *understand others* category but precious little is offered to satisfy the critical educational needs of Aristotle's sage advice that we "know ourselves."

President Ronald Reagan recognized the appropriateness of the old Greek's philosophy when he shared this perspective at the 1986 Presidential Scholars Awards Ceremony: "Loyalty, faithfulness, commitment, courage, patriotism. The ability to distinguish between right and wrong. I hope that these values are as much a part of your life as any calculus course or social science study."

25

Many people recognize too late that personal values and foundational components essential for building meaningful success and creating a worthwhile legacy reside in *knowing ourselves* and in *understanding others.*

Perhaps it's time for a figurative whack upside the head prompting us to observe how much more alike people are than they are different...a whack to motivate acceptance of personal responsibility for our life. It is critically important that thoughtful and decisive attention be directed to fine-tuning—or radically adjusting—our approach to life.

Common Characteristics

Søren Kierkegaard provided the basis for a beautiful analogy in a 19th-century writing illustrating the reason so many people have a "tough" life. He suggested we imagine that geese were like us—they could talk and plan and structure society just as humans do. The geese would have weekly divine worship services and listen intently as the Great High Gander preached powerful, motivating sermons about the wonderful destiny envisioned by the Creator for every bird of every feather. He would marvel that every goose and every gander had been equipped with wings to permit them to fly away to distant regions to accomplish the Creator's purposes.

Every Sunday, the message was the same. Every Sunday, the geese curtsied, and the ganders bowed their heads reverently and enthusiastically honked their understanding and appreciation of the Creator's thoughtfulness. And every Sunday as the congregation dispersed, every goose and every gander *waddled* home!

Why didn't the geese *fly* home? Because in the real world, it's easier to maintain the status quo than deal with the discomfort of change. In spite of knowing how to pursue a better life, they defaulted to playing the Game of Life the same old way, day after day after day.

The Absurd Activities Anomaly

A human frailty exists whereby we know what we should—or should not—do but choose to behave differently. This phenomenon may be called the *Absurd Activities Anomaly* since behavior serving our best interests is often within our range of capability, but we choose to ignore the opportunity. That's so stupid...it's absurd!

One fact about the *Absurd Activities Anomaly* is that sooner or later everyone is affected by it. The Apostle Paul,[4] arguably the most influential Christian in history, personally recognized its impact:

> For what I am doing, I do not understand.
> For what I will to do, that I do not practice,
> but what I hate, that I do.
>
> Romans 7:15

At the other end of the spectrum is a California truck driver who rigged weather balloons to a lawn chair and took a 45-minute ride aloft to 16,000 feet over Metropolitan Los Angeles. When the cold air began causing numbness, he used a pellet gun to burst some of the balloons. The chair drifted downward, controlled only by the gallon jugs of water attached to the sides as ballast, and crashed into a power line. The Federal Aviation Administration was not amused by this lawn chair pilot's afternoon excursion.

Minimizing the *Absurd Activities Anomaly* phenomenon in your life will exponentially increase the probability of reaching your hopes and dreams. The problem is that too often, our rational mind is not in the game.

The Game of Life

Life is sometimes referred to as a game and in many ways, it's a legitimate comparison. For example, in a board game or an athletic contest, choices, or decisions made by the players create a set of circumstances affecting the final outcome. Similarly, your day-to-day choices and decisions result in whether you win or lose—and by how much—in the Game of Life! The beauty of the

Game of Life is that with one small exception, *you* are allowed to make and revise the rules.

The exception is that in organized competitive games, every coach, player, official, and most fans clearly understand the time remaining in the game. Everyone understands that when time runs out, there will be winners and losers...and the result will be final!

The Game of Life is likewise time-bounded for individual players. The difference is that players *do not know* when the final whistle will blow signifying the end of their participation in the game! The uncertainty of life should be an encouragement to proactively live life to its fullest every day.

Some players elect to sit on the bench, watching others enjoy and/or stress out over the game. Others choose to view life as TEGWAR⁵ and strive to manipulate people and events to their own advantage. God's desire is for life to be viewed as a team sport with a central goal of creating and nurturing relationships. *He wants everyone to be an active participant!*

Henry David Thoreau (1817–1862) is said to have summed-up the reality of most people's lives with this observation: "The mass of men lead lives of quiet desperation and go to the grave with their song still in them."

Thoreau is also credited with this stimulating advice: "Go confidently in the direction of your dreams! Live the life you've imagined." Great advice but we must recognize and adhere to the rules and realities of life while pursuing our desired life and legacy.

Realities of Life

We were not born with all the answers and proceed to live a secure life in the light of wisdom and understanding. We were born ignorant, knowing nothing except the stimulus of discomfort which automatically stimulated an attention-getting mechanism.

Transitioning from total ignorance to a storehouse of knowledge and a treasure chest of wisdom requires concentrated time and effort...and a bit of humility. It requires plunging into life, doing what we must do, and experiencing what we must experience.

Plunging into life requires the courage to create personal ripples to be observed by others over extensive time and great distances. The ripples of your life—your personal influence—will directly or indirectly affect many more lives than you can possibly imagine. To plunge or not to plunge is a decision you cannot avoid.

A Smooth Stone
Not to decide is to decide!

Our Common Condition

Every one of us arrived involuntarily on life's scene one day. Uniquely created, we were equipped to survive and thrive for many years, but life's winnowing effects ensure that some thrive and survive longer and more successfully than others.

Each individual arrives on the precipice of life sharing two common characteristics that must be well-managed in the quest of a godly legacy.

1. *Everyone is a "natural born" drifter.* Our natural tendency is to seek the path of least resistance. We are inclined to pass the hours, days—and years—of our lives like a leaf drifting slowly this way and that way, propelled by the influencing winds of circumstance, emotions, and opinions of other people.

   A small percentage were fortunate enough to be born into a nurturing family and taught the value of disciplined behavior and focused planning. However, many were disadvantaged in this respect until we learned through observation, education, or experience that success comes by living like a shot arrow—speeding steadily and consistently toward a defined target for a better life!

2. *Everyone is a "natural born" procrastinator.* Everyone has an innate predisposition to wait for the right moment, a better time, or a more lucrative opportunity. Meanwhile, life—and its opportunities—are passing us by!

> All of us tend to put off living.
> We are all dreaming of some magical rose garden
> over the horizon instead of enjoying the roses
> that are blooming outside our window today.
> —Dale Carnegie[6]

Overwhelmed by the enormity of the moment, plans for our future often receive little attention. Caught up in habitual rituals for daily living, we may lose sight of our ultimate destination. We may become so busy maintaining the status quo that progress toward a better, more rewarding life slows to a crawl and ultimately stagnates.

Quantity of Life vs. Quality of Life

Which is most important, more or better? This question is frequently ignored until age or infirmity begins to affect a person's lifestyle; at which time it becomes supremely important.

The 16th-century French philosopher Montaigne (môn-ten'yu) cast his vote for quality of life. He wisely believed you can live a long physical life but in terms of *really living*, you can completely miss the boat!

Jack London[7] was more expressive in his perspective: "I'd rather be ashes than dust. I would rather that my spark would burn out in a brilliant blaze than be stifled by dry rot. I would rather be a superb meteor, every atom of me in magnificent glow, than a sleepy and permanent planet."

Whichever choice—quantity or quality—best suits your desires, it's important to remember that you are the key player in the personal game of your life.

Voltaire (1694–1778) realistically observed, "Each player must accept the cards life deals him or her. But once they are in hand, he or she alone must decide how to play the cards in order to win the game."

There will never be a better time than today for you to begin developing a game-winning plan. It's so easy to rationalize or make excuses that you must constantly motivate yourself to resist procrastination.

> To be always intending to make a new and better life but never to find time to set about it is as to put off eating and drinking and sleeping from one day to the next until you're dead.
>
> —Og Mandino[8]

There is no better time than this moment to choose—and to live—a life that creates a legacy worth emulating. The key is to accept total responsibility for your life and to make a habit of wise choices.

Today

Today is mine. It is unique.
Nobody in the world has a today exactly like mine.
Today is the sum of my past experience plus my future potential.
Today will become what I *choose* to make it!
I can choose to fill today with joyful moments.
I can saturate today with anxious and worrisome thoughts.
It is my choice...for *today* is mine!
©2007 J. Carl Newell

Now is the time to review the basics of life and consider your future!

Chapter Notes

1. Danish philosopher and theologian, Søren Kierkegaard (1813–1855), wrote extensively about the "emptiness" he observed within Christianity and Danish churches.

2. A character played by actor John Wayne (1907–1979) made a similar statement in the 1947 movie *Sands of Iwo Jima*.

3. Aristotle (384 BC–322 BC) was a Greek philosopher during the Classical period in Ancient Greece. He was the founder of the Lyceum and the Peripatetic school of philosophy. Along with his teacher Plato, he has been called the "Father of Western Philosophy."

4. The Apostle Paul, often considered the most important person after Jesus in the history of Christianity, was likely beheaded by the Romans under Emperor Nero sometime in the summer of AD 68. This quotation is from The Holy Bible, Romans 7:15.

5. *The Exciting Game Without Any Rules* (TEGWAR) is a fictional poker-like card game created by Mark Harris for his 1954 novel, *Bang the Drum Slowly*. The book and subsequent movie (1973) are highly recommended.

6. Dale Carnegie (1888–1955) was one of the earliest self-help gurus. His famous courses focusing on self-improvement and interpersonal skills are still extremely popular.

7. Jack London (1876–1916) is the pseudonym of John Griffith Chaney, an American novelist and short-story writer whose best-known works—among them, *The Call of the Wild* (1903) and *White Fang* (1906)—depict man's basic struggles for survival.

8. Og Mandino (1923–1996) is likely the most widely read inspirational and self-help author in the world today.

Chapter 4
Begin with the Basics

Everything should be made as simple as possible, but not simpler.
—Albert Einstein

John Wooden[1] is legendary—both as player and coach—in NCAA basketball history. More importantly, the ripple effects of his life and legacy positively affects generations of people who never had direct contact with him.

Coach Wooden's unparalleled success as head coach of the UCLA Bruins was largely due to his focus on and building upon the simple basics of the game. The first practice of every season began the same way:

> I'd walk in and there would be these young men who were wonderful players in high school and my first words to them would be, "Today we're going to learn how to put on our socks and shoes. It is important that you pull your socks on just so. Any wrinkle in the sock will cause rubbing that will cause blisters. Blisters keep you from practicing, which keeps you from getting better."[2]

By focusing on the mundane basics of preparation, Coach Wooden taught his players to consider the future while giving attention to the reality of the present. Creating your personal legacy requires the same level of attention to the realities of life. Reality must form the foundation for your beliefs—not wishful thinking, fantasies, or what your friends think.

Reality includes everything that is and has been, whether or not physically observable or comprehensible.

You may mock, criticize, laugh at or disbelieve historical reality but you cannot change it. *It is what it is!* You can accept or ignore reality to your own benefit or peril but either way, a life worth emulating must adhere to these life-changing realities:

Reality: God is eternal. He is, always has been, and will forever be!

"'I am the Alpha and the Omega, the Beginning and the End,' says the Lord, 'who is and who was and who is to come, the Almighty'" (Revelation 1:8, NIV).

Jesus Christ is the same yesterday, today, and forever (Hebrews 13:8, NIV).

Reality: God used ordinary people to transcribe His message to the world. Over a period of approximately 1600 years, thirty-six individuals[3] of diverse backgrounds and experience were obedient to His divine inspiration. The result of their labor was the Bible, a thorough, complete, and error-free communication from God to mankind.

All Scripture is given by inspiration of God, and is profitable for doctrine, for reproof, for correction, for instruction in righteousness (2 Timothy 3:16, KJV).

Reality: God is love!

He who does not love does not know God, because God is love (1 John 4:8, NIV).

Reality: God loves you!

In this the love of God was manifested toward us, that God has sent His only begotten Son into the world, that we might live through Him. In this is love, not that we loved God, but that He loved us and sent His Son to be the propitiation for our sins.

1 John 4:9-10

Reality: God created everyone equal and loves everyone equally!

For God does not show favoritism (Romans 2:11, NIV).

For God so loved the world that he gave his only begotten Son, that whoever believes in him should not perish but have eternal life (John 3:16).

Reality: God's love for you is sufficient and everlasting!

For I am persuaded that neither death nor life, nor angels nor principalities nor powers, nor things present nor things to come, nor height nor depth, nor any other created thing, shall be able to separate us from the love of God which is in Christ Jesus our Lord.

Romans 8:38-39 (KJV)

Let your conduct be without covetousness; be content with such things as you have. For He Himself has said, "I will never leave you nor forsake you."

Hebrews 13:5

Creating a legacy worthy of emulation requires facing the reality of God and examining your personal beliefs. *What do you believe?*

Your Belief System

Life is *essentially* binary. There are varying shades of "maybe" along the way to life's decisions but ultimately, everything becomes either/or, right or wrong, good or bad, will or won't. *Maybe* is a convenient place to pause—briefly or indefinitely—for you to gather more facts or to wallow serenely in procrastination. Either way, the ultimate decision will be yea or nay. *Not to decide is to decide.*

Belief is *absolutely* binary. The resting place of maybe is non-existent in your belief system. There is no middle ground when considering these realities:

- You believe God is who He claims to be...or you don't.
- You believe Jesus is who He claims to be...or you don't.
- You believe the Bible is God's inerrant Word...or you don't.

Since God cannot be seen with physical eyes, some people struggle with believing the reality of His eternal existence. This observation by Ashleigh

Brilliant[4] is consistent with my personal beliefs: "The existence of God has already been proven to my satisfaction by the existence of everything else."

Belief in the veracity of the Bible is required to accept as fact that Jesus is the Son of God and willfully submitted to an agonizing death by crucifixion to atone for our sins.

If you choose to disagree with or flat-out disbelieve any portion of Scripture, you are in essence claiming to be God. And you are not.

Intentionally responding to God's reality by setting aside pride and accepting Jesus as your personal Savior is necessary for you to fulfill your role in the Game of Life.

Your Personal Reality

Not every eligible basketball player opted to accept Coach Wooden's guidance and leadership and become part of his team. Those who chose to opt-in to the UCLA basketball program had to have *faith* in Coach Wooden, *believe* he had their best interests at heart, *trust* his judgment and *obey* his game plan. Everyone who wishes to join God's team must demonstrate the same attributes toward Him.

Here is a phenomenal truth: God wants to have a personal relationship with you. Affirming that every person is eligible and qualified to join his team, He emphasizes that He "...is not willing that *any* should perish but that all should come to repentance" (2 Peter 3:9, emphasis added).[5]

Even though God wants everyone everywhere to be on His winning team, some will choose to opt-out. Everyone is eligible to accept Jesus as their personal Savior and receive the Holy Spirit as their Life Coach, but some willfully choose to reject Him. Many more procrastinate until it's too late. *Not to decide is to decide.*

Perhaps you occasionally feel an emptiness or incompleteness within yourself and are unable to identify the cause. An assertion frequently attributed to

Blaise Pascale[6] could be a plausible explanation:

> There is a God-shaped vacuum in the heart of every person, and it can never be filled by any created thing. It can only be filled by God, made known through Jesus Christ.

Just as UCLA's basketball players demonstrated faith in Coach Wooden by believing him and his promises for the future, you must demonstrate the same faith in the Son of God to become "complete."

The Bible provides assurance that everyone who wants to be on God's team will be:

> "If you openly declare that Jesus is Lord and believe in your heart that God raised him from the dead, you *will be* saved" (Romans 10:9, NLT, emphasis added).

> For whoever calls on the name of the LORD *shall* be saved (Romans 10:13, emphasis added).

Truth is very narrow—there is just one way to have a personal relationship with God. Jesus said, "I am *the* way, *the* truth and *the* life. *No one* comes to the Father except through Me" (John 14:6, emphasis added).

The simplest way to create a new and everlasting reality for yourself is by having a heartfelt conversation with God, i.e. a prayer similar to this one:

> Dear God, I am a sinner. I cannot live a truly worthwhile life without your help. I believe Jesus Christ is your Son and that He died on the cross for my sin. I believe you raised Him from the dead. Right now, I accept Jesus as my personal Lord and Savior. Thank you for forgiving me, for saving me, and for assuring that I will have eternal life with you in Heaven. Amen

After that is settled, you are a Christian—a Christ follower—and will begin to desire the habit of trusting and obeying Him. As you grow in your relationship with God, you will begin to see yourself through His eyes and realize that living the Christian life is a process.

You will have a new nature but won't automatically think all good thoughts, express all the right attitudes, and give up all bad habits. You can expect to experience doubts and uncertainty as you begin your Christian life—these are tools of Satan—but you can rely on God's assurance that you are eternally secure under his protection.

- *God assures you that your sins have been forgiven:*

  You were dead because of your sins and because your sinful nature was not yet cut away. Then God made you alive with Christ for he forgave all our sins. He canceled the record of the charges against us and took it away by nailing it to the cross.

  Colossians 2:13-14 (NLT)

- *God assures you that Jesus Christ has come into your life:* "When I am raised to life again, you will know that I am in my Father, and you are in me, and I am in you" (John 14:20, NLT).

- *God assures you that you have eternal life:* "I have written this to you who believe in the name of the Son of God, so that you may know you have eternal life" (John 5:13, NLT).

With reassurance of your Christian status intact, remember that God has maintained clear and specific expectations of His people throughout the eons of history:

> ...the LORD has told you what is good, and this is what he *requires* of you: to do what is right, to love mercy, and to walk humbly with your God.[7]

As a new Believer, you will want to immediately begin seeking to understand God's purposes and desires for your life. He will give you knowledge as you prayerfully seek guidance every day through prayer and reading the Bible.

While there are many excellent Bibles available, my personal favorite is the New King James Version (NKJV) as presented by *The Charles F. Stanley Life Principles Bible.* Dr. Stanley[8] provides easy to understand biblical explanations for many of life's problems and gives practical insight into how to apply God's Word to everyday life.

CAUTION! You need to recognize that Satan works overtime in planting seeds of doubt in the mind of new Christians. The continued impulse to do things contrary to what you know is "right" may cause you to wonder if you *really are* a Christian. Just remember that God patiently understands the process you must go through to replace *old* habits with *new* habits. Your responsibility is to continually say "no" to sin and "yes" to God until your natural impulses coincide with what you know will please Him.

A Smooth Stone
A yes to one thing is always a no to something else.

Recognizable change may be slow in coming but will become evident as you trust God to give you new desires and habits. Your new life and new behavior will distinctly communicate the new you! Meanwhile, you will be reaping the wonderful benefits of *God's Rewards Program.*

God's Rewards Program

Rewards and loyalty programs are so commonplace in today's society that people often feel ripped-off unless their purchase includes rewards points that will accumulate into a free *something* in the future. Depending on the merchant, points may be redeemed for a free chicken sandwich or a round-trip airline ticket to almost anywhere in the world. However, the glitziest commercial loyalty program is pitifully puny compared to *God's Rewards Program.*

God's program is uniquely designed to be unencumbered by small-print rules and regulations. Requirements to qualify for His program are clearly and simply stated in the Bible:

> And it is impossible to please God without *faith*. Anyone who wants to come to him must *believe* that God exists and that he *rewards* those who sincerely *seek* him.[9]

When you demonstrated faith and belief in God by acknowledging your sinful condition and accepting Jesus as your personal Savior, you were automatically enrolled in God's Rewards Program!

Bible scholars have identified thousands of promises God made to reveal wonderful blessings and opportunities for Christians. God is absolutely trustworthy, and His promises are irrevocable, but it is important to remember that many promises are conditional upon personal obedience.

As a program member, you qualify for most of His promises! No additional action required! Your membership will never expire and cannot be canceled or revoked. In fact, not that you would want to, but not even you can cancel your membership!

KEY POINT: Eternal life in Heaven is a *gift*, not a *reward!*

A Worthwhile Lesson

Live life with the end in mind! Grantland Rice[10] penned this eloquent end-of-life truth:

> For when the One Great Scorer comes to mark against your name, He writes not that you won or lost, but how you played the game!

Unless you have a personal relationship with Jesus, your legacy will be a dud! Some people may find temporary happiness and success by following your example but be deprived of indescribable blessings both now and throughout eternity.

Chapter Notes

1. John Wooden (1910–2010) was a three-time All-American basketball player (Purdue) who became legendary as head coach of the UCLA Bruins (1948–1975). He led the Bruins to ten NCAA National Championships. During one stretch, UCLA won an NCAA men's basketball record 88 consecutive games. In spite of his legendary status as a coach, John Wooden

seemed proudest to be a teacher, mentor, and friend.

2. This quotation is from *Success* magazine, August/September 2008, pages 92ff.

3. Source: John Knox Cummings, *Confessing Christ*, p14, Great Commission Publications, 1992.

4. Ashleigh Brilliant (b. 1933) is an author and syndicated cartoonist born in London. He became a naturalized United States citizen in 1969 and is best known for his syndicated *Pot-Shots*, single-panel illustrations with one-line humorous remarks.

5. Some people believe that because God does not want anyone to perish, He will not allow a person to spend eternity in Hell. This logic is flawed because everyone has the free will to accept or reject Jesus. God emphatically states that Jesus is the *only* way to escape Hell and receive eternal life in Heaven: "He who believes in Him is not condemned; but he who does not believe is condemned already, because he has not believed in the name of the only begotten Son of God." (John 3:18).

6. Blaise Pascal (1623–1662) was a French mathematician, physicist, and religious philosopher. This quotation has evolved over the years from a concept presented in his writing *Pensées*, a defense of the Christian religion published eight years after his death.

7. To be a "good Christian" requires more than simply following standard religious practices. God wants you to follow the Holy Spirit's guidance in making wise life choices every day. Source: The Bible, Micah 6:8, NLT (emphasis added).

8. Charles F. Stanley (b. 1932) is the senior pastor of First Baptist Church, Atlanta, Georgia. Dr. Stanley is the founder and president of *In Touch Ministries* and served two one-year terms as president of the Southern Baptist Convention.

9. As your faith grows, your desire to seek and obey God's commands will increase. When His direction for your life seems unreasonable, impossible, or just doesn't make any sense to you, remember that He sees the end from the beginning and *always* has your best interests in mind. Source: Hebrews 11:6 NLT, (emphasis added).

10. Grantland Rice (1880–1954) was an early 20th-century sports columnist and author who established himself as one of America's leading sports authorities.

Chapter 5
Look to the Future

You cannot escape the responsibility
of tomorrow by evading it today.
—Abraham Lincoln

Things that don't change tend to remain the same!

History and memory are vitally important to unlocking your lasting legacy. Lessons buried within your past contain useful material for strengthening the foundation of your future.

If you want to keep on getting what you've been getting, just keep on doing what you've been doing! If you want something different—and more satisfying—you'll need to review and assess the behavior that brought you to this point in life.

Personal habits intertwined with the rigors of everyday life often cause us to miss the mark of behaving in ways we know would be pleasing to God. A life of positive influence and a far-reaching legacy requires intentionality toward the future.

One incontrovertible fact often ignored or overlooked is, "I am 100% responsible for the choices and decisions that define my life." Your life is the composite of a lifetime of outside influences coupled with personal decisions.

Without being unduly harsh, ask yourself, "Am I OK with my life 'as is' or is there something that needs to be cleaned up or improved?" No matter where you've come from or where you're headed, there's likely at least one area in your life needing remedial attention.

I discovered a simple poem many years ago that gently and subtly suggests the importance of reviewing personal priorities and behavior in light of God's plans and desires for my life.

The Broom

God knocked on the door of my heart one day
    And I looked for a place to hide.
My soul was cluttered and choked with debris
    And things were untidy inside.

There were tasks neglected, long overdue;
    Cobwebs to be brushed from the wall.
Rugs to be shaken and windows cleaned up...
    I had not expected His call!

I stood with my hand on the latch of the door
    And gazed at the mess in the room.
When I opened the door, my soul blushed to see,
    God had left on my doorstep, a broom!
(Author Unknown)

God has given each of us a metaphorical broom. He expects us to sweep out inconsistency and disobedience from within the nooks and crannies of our life to make room for a better future. Reviewing your past in light of current knowledge will help you develop an enviable legacy, but you must avoid getting hung-up on past failures and disappointments.

Don't cry over spilled milk! This old adage suggests that being upset over something that has already happened and cannot be changed is futile. Rather than being disheartened by "spilled milk"—earlier mistakes and failures caused by bad decisions—be encouraged by this twist on its message: *Spilled milk doesn't matter as long as you still have the cow.*

Back to the Basics

It was July of 1961. Still reeling from a heartbreaking defeat six months earlier, the 38 members of the Green Bay Packers football team gathered for the first day of training camp.

44

After squandering a lead late in the fourth quarter, the Packers had lost the 1960 NFL Championship game to the Philadelphia Eagles. Through the remainder of Winter and all Spring, these athletes eagerly anticipated making amends to their fans...and to each other. To a man, they were ready to hustle onto the field and strenuously begin working toward winning the championship.

Their coach—Vince Lombardi[1]—had a different idea. The legendary coach began a tradition that day of opening the first day of every season's training camp in an unusual manner. He chose to assume that every player's football memory was a blank slate—containing no awareness of previous disappointments and failures. Rather than moving immediately to the practice field, Lombardi held a football in his right hand and said, "Gentlemen, this is a football."

Vince Lombardi was coaching professional athletes who had come within minutes of winning the NFL's most coveted prize. And yet, he treated them as beginners by taking them back to the basic fundamentals of the game. Lombardi recognized that no matter how disappointing and regrettable the past may be, it cannot be undone, revised, or rewritten.

He also knew that a critical review of individual strengths and weaknesses could be a springboard to future success. His message is that positively focusing on behavior modification will lead to future success, happiness, and satisfaction in life.

Following Coach Lombardi's approach to overcoming the sting of past failures, you can go back to the basics of life and focus on improving the quality of your future.

Where's Your Focus?

Every second of your life is spent at the intersection of the ever-increasing past and the never-ending future.

Although it's impossible to reside even one nanosecond in the past or the future, we often sacrifice the present by fretting over unalterable history and unknowable tomorrows.

In essence, we crucify ourselves between two thieves—*regret* for our past and *fear* of the future. Unwittingly authorizing regret for past behavior interferes with the current moment's possibilities and diminishes the quality and potential of our future. Similarly, the *fear* of unborn tomorrows robs us of today's joy and happiness.

Regretting our past—which cannot be changed—and worrying about events that may never become reality leaves many of God's intended blessings withering on the vine.

In His omniscience, God knew we would be suckered into behavior driven by this *Absurd Anomaly* and graciously provided wise counsel for dealing with its futility:

> The Apostle Paul shared his philosophy: "One thing I do: forgetting what lies behind and straining forward to what lies ahead, I press on toward the goal for the prize of the upward call of God in Christ Jesus." (Philippians 3:13b-14, ESV).

> Jesus gave this advice, "Don't worry about tomorrow, for tomorrow will bring its own worries. Today's trouble is enough for today." (Matthew 6:34, NLT).

Compartmentalize Your Focus

United States Navy warships are engineered and constructed to be internally watertight. In the event flooding occurs, watertight doors designed to withstand intense water pressure from either side are in place to prevent the passage of water between compartments.

In a 1913 speech to Yale University students, Sir William Osler[2]—one of the world's most influential physicians— drew an analogy between a ship's watertight door protection and the *Absurd Anomaly* of focusing on the past and fearing the future. He suggested creating "day-tight compartments" using metaphorical iron doors to shut out the pressures of the past and shutoff anxiety about the future. These day-tight doors keep the pressures of yesterday and tomorrow from interfering with today's opportunities.

Dr. Osler was not suggesting we make zero effort in preparing for the future. His idea was that focusing *today's* mental energy on *today's* activities and opportunities will ensure our best possible future.

His lesson gains further clarity as you recall The Lord's Prayer: "Give us this day our daily bread."[3] Jesus recommended we ask only for *today's* bread without complaining about *yesterday's* stale bread and without worrying whether *tomorrow's* bread will be fresh and sufficient.

A step-by-step process for implementing Dr. Osler's philosophy is not available, but the idea of compartmentalizing daily activities and spending less time fretting about the past and fearing the future is a good one.

Resolve to act today—and every day—to accomplish the things most important to your success. Following this discipline, you will develop invaluable habits for creating a noteworthy legacy.

Looking to a predictably unpredictable future, you may be certain it will include a mixture of adversity and pain. Fortunately, God gifted you with innate abilities and the flexibility to create plans for your desired future in spite of the uncertainty of life.

Adversity is Inevitable

Everyone has experienced the ache of sadness and anxiety when adversity turned life upside-down. Remembering God has a plan for your life and legacy will help you maintain perspective and effectively manage the emotion of discouragement.

A Smooth Stone
Adversity is inevitable but discouragement is optional!

We know blessings are gifts from God, but He also uses adversity to get our attention. He allows difficulties to enter our lives to deepen our relationship with Him and to be a blessing of encouragement to others.

> Enjoy prosperity while you can, but when hard times strike, realize that both come from God. Remember that nothing is certain in this life. (Ecclesiastes 7:14, NLT).

When life throws you a curve, recognize that adversity comes in many shapes and forms. Sometimes, it's like a speed bump...you see it, slow down, and make a minor adjustment. Sometimes, it is simply a stumbling block...you hit it, bounce off, learn a lesson, and get on with life.

However, adversity sometimes appears as a bona fide, overwhelming giant, immune to all your hand-wringing and gut-wrenching whining and complaining.

No matter the significance or origin of a mammoth-sized problem or whether it crashes unexpectedly into your life or arrives quietly, its basis is always a *fact* or a *problem*. The fundamental difference is that a *fact* is a fact and consequently, has no solution whereas a *problem* always has at least one solution.

Don't waste time and energy trying to solve facts. Instead, invest your resources in identifying and focusing on problems that need to be solved. Not every problem must be resolved; some will dissolve and disappear without your intervention.

When the mind-bending stress of problems seem overwhelming and the future looks bleak, talk to Jesus—the ultimate Problem Solver. Look into the Bible; it contains the answers to all of life's problems.

Three steps for climbing out of the slippery Pit of Adversity:

1. *Accept the truth of Scripture and act on its promises!*

Give your burdens to the LORD, and he will take care of you. He will not permit the godly to slip and fall. (Psalm 55:22, NLT).

2. *Speak your burdens out loud.* Tell God exactly which problems you find insurmountable. Share your desired outcomes with Him. Ask for grace to accept and abide by His will for your life.

3. *Personalize and verbally claim Scriptural truth:*

"I know and believe that your grace is sufficient for me, your strength is made perfect in my weakness and that my faith will be strengthened through adversity." (*See* 2 Corinthians 12:9).

A Smooth Stone
Every problem has a prayer solution.

Although Mother Teresa[4] constantly faced dismal circumstances, she chose a wonderful attitude toward adversity rather than submitting to discouragement. She mused, "I know God will not give me anything I can't handle. I just wish that He didn't trust me so much."

Not unlike Mother Teresa, Christians today can be comforted and encouraged by God's promise to Joshua as he became Israel's leader:

And the LORD, He is the One who goes before you. He will be with you. He will not leave you nor forsake you; do not fear nor be dismayed. (Deuteronomy 31:8).

The Apostle Paul provided assurance that God uses *everything*—including painful experiences for our benefit:

And we know that *all* things work together for good to those who love God, to those who are the called according to His purpose. (Romans 8:28, emphasis added).

Mark Twain[5]— a keen observer of life and its commonality among the masses—is said to have confessed, "I am an old man and have known a great many troubles, but most of them have never happened."

Likewise, many of *your* worries and concerns will never become a reality but remember, God has a knack for using both real and perceived problems to your ultimate advantage.

If you're paying attention to life, the passage of time will teach you to appreciate Twain's confession and O. Henry's observation that "Life is made up of sobs, sniffles, and smiles, with sniffles predominating."[6]

Pain is Inevitable

Life is a never-ending series of choices usually intended to improve some aspect of your personal life. Every decision comes with a price to be paid, i.e. each requires a selection from the binary menu. You must make a choice: *do or don't do, do it now or do it later.*

A Smooth Stone
Unwise choices often create personal pain!

Major decisions involve accepting, rejecting or revising a belief or a behavior and may be accompanied by:

    a. the pain of discipline, or
    b. the pain of regret.

Making a wise decision and sticking with it may require enduring the *pain of discipline* for a period of time but is usually followed by significant personal benefits. Unwise choices or neglecting to make important decisions may lead to the lasting *pain of regret.*

By unwittingly initiating a goal-setting process a long time ago, I learned the value of sacrificing current pleasure for future benefits:

It was Friday, December 17, 1965, onboard USS *Fidelity.*[7]

During a casual conversation in the Radio Shack about the health effects of smoking, I suggested that I, Danny and Eddie—the other Radiomen—quit smoking. I instinctively realized that we could achieve success by setting a specific, time-bounded, measurable goal, and proposed a 30-day test.

We each agreed to put $5 in the safe, smoke one last cigarette, and see who could make it 30 days without a smoke. The money would go to whoever lasted the entire 30 days. We lit our final cig and puffed away; mine was a Camel, smoked down until the ash was burning my lips.

Having been a pack-a-day smoker for eight years, I began feeling the *pain of discipline* within the first hour and remember thinking, "If I can only make it until tomorrow, I can make it!"

Day by agonizing day, the month finally passed, and amazingly, all three shipmates reached the goal of 30 days without a cigarette. Congratulating each other, we pocketed our five bucks, and went back to work. At around 30 days and 20 minutes, Eddie took off to the Mess Deck to mooch a smoke; Danny lasted about a week but that Camel was my last cigarette.

Although little—if any—thought was given to the ultimate effects of my decision, the *pain of discipline* was clearly the catalyst for providing life-changing benefits.

For example, *Google* just calculated that as of the moment of this writing, I have been a non-smoker for 19,747 days! A simple extrapolation shows:

1. 394,940 cigarettes have gone unsmoked.
2. Assuming ten drags per cigarette, I have avoided 3,949,400 nicotine-polluted breaths of air.
3. Conservatively assuming a cost of $1.00 per pack,[8] I have avoided spending $19,747 on cigarettes.

What if I had opted out of participating in the 30-day experiment? At a minimum, I would have:

- Smoked 394,940 cigarettes and inhaled at least 3,949,400 grossly impure breaths of air.
- Essentially lit a match and burned up $20,000.
- Tacitly agreed to put my future health in jeopardy.
- Missed the opportunity—*which I ignored!*—to invest the $1.00 saved each day. If that one dollar-a-day had been invested each day at an average 2% interest rate, its value today would be $34,957.[9]

Every wise decision you make is for the benefit of yourself or someone else and is in obedience to God. The *pain of discipline* associated with these decisions is a temporary investment that produces long-term blessings and benefits.

Conversely, unwise decisions and willful disobedience to God creates a debit from your future well-being while adding a measure of the *pain of regret*. Deferring obedience to God can lead to opportunities missed forever and unresolvable regrets. *Not to decide is to decide!*

A Smooth Stone
Consider the alternatives, then choose wisely!

Temptation's Pernicious Nature

I can resist everything except temptation. These words of Oscar Wilde could be truthfully spoken by millions of people today.[10]

Temptation makes a compelling presentation to your ego, senses, and fantasies. Its allure and promises of pleasure, social acceptance and perhaps financial gain is enticing, but a stranglehold of undesirable habits eager to embrace you is always lurking beneath its beautiful veneer.

You must be aware of temptation's subtle message: "You can pay me now or you can pay me later." The implicit idea is you can endure the *pain of discipline* by resisting the temptation now or risk being inextricably linked to the *pain of regret* in the future.

Following temptation's pathway to immoral, sinful, and unwise habits and behavior requires a conscious decision and creates a nagging conscience within a Christian. The best antidote to assuage a guilty conscience is to seek and obey God's wisdom.

When you *know* that accepting temptation's bidding will displease God, you may be encouraged and strengthened by this Scripture:

> The temptations in your life are no different from what others experience. And God is faithful. He will not allow the temptation to be more than you can stand. When you are tempted, he will show you a way out so that you can endure. (1 Corinthians 10:13, NLT).

Saying "*No!*" to a sinful temptation is equivalent to saying an obedient "*Yes!*" to God. Emphatically resisting temptation requires willfully accepting the *pain of discipline* by consciously deciding to obey God:

> But don't just listen to God's word. You must do what it says. Otherwise, you are only fooling yourselves. (James 1:22, NLT).

The Bible gives this step-by-step process to avoid the pitfalls and snares of temptation:

> *Resist the devil* and he will flee from you. *Draw near to God* and He will draw near to you. (James 4:7b, 8a, emphasis added).

The courage and determination necessary to effectively live the Christian life and create your worthwhile legacy is available through the assurance of God's Word:

> I can do all things through Christ who strengthens me. (Philippians 4:13).

How can the chains of yesterday's habits that prevent you from living a life worth emulating be broken? Second Peter 1:3 promises, "His divine power has given to us all things that pertain to life and godliness."

God is eager to provide the wisdom and power necessary to create your desired legacy. *Work with Him!*

Chapter Notes

1. Vince Lombardi (1913–1970) was a legendary NFL football coach and executive. The Packers' loss to Philadelphia was instrumental in beginning his reign as one of the all-time greatest football coaches. He never lost in the playoffs again and never coached a team with a losing record. Lombardi posted a 96-34-6 record plus a 9-1 post-season record.

2. Sir William Osler (1849–1919) was a renowned Canadian physician and one of the four founding professors of Johns Hopkins Hospital. Dr. Osler's Yale University speech on April 20, 1913, was titled *A Way of Life.*

3. The Lord's Prayer is recorded in Matthew 6:9-13.

4. Mary Teresa Bojaxhiu (1910–1997) better known as Mother Teresa, was an Albanian-Indian Roman Catholic nun and missionary to the sick and poor in Calcutta, India. She was awarded the Nobel Peace Prize in 1979, and was canonized as a saint by Pope Francis on September 4, 2016.

5. Mark Twain (1835–1910) was the pen name of Samuel Langhorne Clemens, one of America's foremost humorists, writers, and entrepreneurs.

6. William Sydney Porter (1862–1910) was an American short story writer better known by his pen name, O. Henry. This quotation is from *The Gift of the Magi.*

7. USS *Fidelity* (MSO 443) was an Ocean Minesweeper, a wooden ship with a length of 172' and a beam of 35'. The *Fidelity* was in active service from January 1955 to May 1989.

8. Camel cigarettes purchased tax free on Navy ships in the 1960's cost $1.00 for a carton, one dime per pack. The average price for a pack of

Camels during 2019 was $5.51.

9. The future value of daily savings was computed by the *Daily Savings Calculator* at https://ffcalcs.com/daily_savings

10. Oscar Wilde (1854–1900) was an author, poet, and playwright. This quotation is from Wilde's 1892 comedy, *Lady Windermere's Fan.*

Chapter 6
The Cosmic Coach

What comes from the heart goes to the heart.
—Samuel Taylor Coleridge[1]

The life coaching industry is reporting record revenues worldwide as more and more people sign-up for individual sessions. Many upwardly mobile people and others who just want a better life, hire coaches to help identify personal strengths and weaknesses, and provide guidance in goal setting and planning.

A competent coach will figuratively hold your hand while sharing ideas, knowledge, and encouragement. Each session's thoughtful interactions may be helpful and bolster confidence but whether the end results are minimal or monumental depends on the coach's ability to motivate *you* to motivate *yourself.*

Amazingly, you can save money and have 24/7 access to a unique Inner Coach who not only shares wisdom but *is* wisdom! *The Holy Spirit is eager to be your Inner Coach!*

He wants to actively participate in your life through a deep and never-ending relationship. Rather than being pushy and forcing His desires, the Holy Spirit will gently guide you toward an enhanced relationship with Him:

Draw near to God and He will draw near to you. (James 4:8a).

The intensity of your relationship with God will determine your quality of life and in turn, the likelihood you will live a life worth following and creating a legacy worth emulating. The degree to which you *choose* to "draw near" to God defines the robustness of your relationship.

A Smooth Stone
Whoever values a relationship least determines its depth.

57

Frequent communication sessions with your Inner Coach are necessary to obtain the wisdom, encouragement, and power to live a godly life. You should initiate contact with God often—at least daily—and always be prepared for Him to contact you when you least expect it!

No matter who initiates the meeting, your life will either be *superficial* or *supernatural* depending on the effectiveness of your personal participation.

Celestial Communications

How fast is fast?

The human voice travels at nearly 13 miles per minute. Light travels at an incredible speed of 11,176,920 miles per minute...186,282 miles per second!

Amazingly, when compared to the speed of our communication with God, the speed of light is as slow as a turtle on crutches! Personal meetings with your Inner Coach transcend all measurement of speed...it is instantaneous!

Five channels comprise the celestial communication network:
- Praise
- Prayer
- God's Word
- Inspiration
- Synchronicity

A Reason to Praise

Were you born in the United States of America? If so, you were born standing on third base in the Game of Life. Most others born throughout the world on your birthdate entered the game fidgeting in the batter's box with two strikes against them.

Americans have been blessed with *so much for so long* that we are often unconsciously ungrateful. While average Americans are reluctant to consciously praise God "from Whom all blessings flow," scores of intelligent people all over the world willingly risk *everything* for the slimmest possibility of becoming a United States citizen.

Everybody likes to receive praise—even God! Praising God is an act of the will—*a personal choice*—flowing from a heart filled with awe and reverence for our Creator. God loves it when we consciously praise Him for the innumerable blessings so often taken for granted.

Jesus told about a young man who had everything...a loving father, a good home, and a bright future. Nevertheless, he was so self-centered and unappreciative that he chose a lifestyle that distanced himself from his father's love and the blessings of family and home. This prodigal son abused his father's love. *See* Luke 15:11-32.

If the definition of prodigal is expanded to include an attitude of casual indifference to God, then I—*and possibly you*—might fit the description. When we try to bend God's rules and end up breaking them, we become a prodigal child. Can you identify with any prodigal attitudes described in this poem?

The Prodigal

When I'm a prodigal, lean grocer's shelves aggravate me.
But when I am in my Father's will,
I remember millions hungering for just one slice of bread,
while I could buy a hundred *loaves* today.
Ah, God! You're so good to me!

When I'm a prodigal, a child's incessant questions irritate me.
But when I'm in my Father's will,
I am reminded children are born with an expansive but empty database
and they ask *me* questions out of respect for my wisdom.
Ah, God! You're so good to me!

When I'm a prodigal, people—even friends—can be so annoying!
But when I'm in sync with my Father's will,
I remember He places people in my path for a purpose; so
I may be a blessing to them or they may be a blessing to me!
Ah, God! You're so good to me!

When I'm a prodigal, I see our flag as just a colored rag.
But when I'm in sync with my Father's will,
the Stars and Stripes remind me of sons and daughters who will never
come home again;
those who died so I can breathe the fresh air of freedom.
Ah, God! You're so good to me!

When I'm a prodigal, I'm so self-centered... it's all about me!
But when I'm in sync with my Father's will,
I realize that I'm a small—*but important*—part of His plan,
and walking close to Him, my life is an incredible journey.
Ah, God! You're *so very good* to me!
©2007 J. Carl Newell

We should praise God every day in our own way or by following the rationale and example of this psalmist:

I will praise You, for I am fearfully and wonderfully made.
Marvelous are Your works, and that my soul knows very well.
(Psalm 139:14).

The Awesome Power of Prayer

Prayer is the language that connects us to the Spiritual world. Since the Spiritual world is the source of power, peace, joy, and everything else the physical world needs, it is essential that we learn to speak the language.

Great news! The perfect communicator and interpreter—the Holy Spirit—resides in the heart of every Christian and through the language of prayer, connects God's heart to our human spirit.

When we're troubled and simply don't know what to say or how to say it, the Holy Spirit steps in and communicates our concerns to the Father. The Apostle Paul explained the process this way:

> And the Holy Spirit helps us in our weakness. For example, we don't know what God wants us to pray for. But the Holy Spirit prays for us with groanings that cannot be expressed in words. And the Father who knows all hearts knows what the Spirit is saying, for the Spirit pleads for us believers in harmony with God's own will. (Romans 8:26-27, NLT).

God loves every person more deeply than the most devoted father loves his children. He is vitally interested in your concerns, desires, and needs. He wants you to stay in touch with Him and is eager to actively involve you in resolving problems and in pouring blessings into the lives of others.

> The earnest prayer of a righteous person has great power and produces wonderful results. (James 5:16b, NLT).

Our Creator wants us to communicate with Him and promises to listen when we call. The question is, "Will we listen to Him?" And more importantly, "Will we obey?" A generation ago, Christians encouraged each other to pray by sharing the adage, "Prayer changes things." A more accurate rendering and one worth remembering is:

A Smooth Stone
Prayer changes people. People change things.

Prayer is perhaps the most important habit a Christian can develop. It does not have to be difficult and complicated. Prayer is something that *any* Christian *anywhere* can do at *any time.*

General George S. Patton,[2] arguably the most successful battlefield commander during World War II, was known and respected for his toughness, discipline, and self-sacrifice. His tough-guy persona and reputation overshadowed an important component of his life—his faith in God and belief in the effectiveness of prayer.

61

This amazing incident graphically illustrates Patton's faith in God and in the power of prayer:[3]

> In December 1944, Patton's Third Army was bogged down in Belgium. The enemy was only part of the problem; terrible weather—incessant rain, thick fog and floods were making advance nearly impossible.
>
> Summoned to Patton's office the morning of December 8, Msgr. James H. O'Neill—Chief Chaplain of the Third Army—received an unexpected order. He was directed to write a prayer for the troops to use in asking God to intervene in their plight.
>
> O'Neill recorded Patton's words of instruction: "We've got to get not only the chaplains but every man in the Third Army to pray. We must ask God to stop these rains. These rains are that margin that hold defeat or victory. If we all pray, it will be like what Dr. Carrel said [the allusion was to a press quote some days previously when Dr. Alexis Carrel, one of the foremost scientists, described prayer "as one of the most powerful forms of energy man can generate"], it will be like plugging in on a current whose source is in Heaven. I believe that prayer completes that circuit. It is power."
>
> Within hours, the chaplain was inspired to type this prayer on a 5" X 3" filing card:
>
>> Almighty and most merciful Father, we humbly beseech Thee, of Thy great goodness, to restrain these immoderate rains with which we have had to contend. Grant us fair weather for Battle. Graciously hearken to us as soldiers who call upon Thee that, armed with Thy power, we may advance from victory to victory, and crush the oppression and wickedness of our enemies and establish Thy justice among men and nations

At Patton's command, 250,000 copies of the Prayer Card (including Christmas greetings to the troops) were printed and distributed within days. On December 19, Patton moved his divisions northward toward the enemy and the prayer was answered!

On December 20, to the consternation of the Germans and the delight of the Americans, the rain and fog ceased and was followed by days of bright clear skies and perfect flying weather. The Third Army received tremendous air support for days on end and was totally victorious at the Battle of the Bulge.

General Patton and his soldiers prayed for fair weather for fighting the battle. *They got it!*

Whether your problem, need, or desire is big or small, don't put off bringing it to Jesus. He has the compassion, understanding, and power to fix any problem you will ever face, and He always has time for you. You never have to wait in line or leave a Voicemail...he is always available!

A Smooth Stone
Prayer should be your first resource, not your last resort.

Strengthen your friendship with Him by initiating a brief chat as you prepare for each day. Please free to use or revise this simple morning prayer to meet your needs.

A Morning Prayer

This is Your day, Lord.
Please help me to want what You want
and choose an attitude that blesses others.
Fill my mind with Your thoughts
and make me immune to harmful temptations.
I ask You to speak to my heart today
and show me what I'm supposed to do.

This is Your day, Lord, help me use it wisely.
Amen

Jesus is not only readily available when you're in distress and worried about someone or something specific, He assures us that He is a reliable and dependable friend:

"If you abide in Me, and My words abide in you, you will ask what you desire, and it shall be done for you." (John 15:7).

Don't miss the keyword in the first part of Jesus' statement. He pointedly states that *if* His words are permanently etched in your heart and mind, you will never ask for something inconsistent with His will for your life.

God's Word Speaks

The Bible is a *spiritual* book written by a *spiritual* being to *spiritual* beings. Since you are a spiritual being having a physical experience, its truths were written especially for you.

The Bible contains the answer to every question and the solution to every problem you will encounter as you seek to understand and fulfill His purpose for your life. God's Word will change your life...*if you let it!*

Jesus said to the people who believed in him, "You are truly my disciples if you remain faithful to my teachings. And you will know the truth, and the truth will set you free." (John 8:31-32, NLT).

Simple logic dictates that familiarity with Scripture is necessary for you to *know* and *obey* His teachings. Acknowledge and obey Jesus' expectations... and be released from the grip and guilt of personal sin!

A Smooth Stone
Only the truth you know can set you free.

The Bible provides the wisdom necessary for living a life worth following and creating a lasting legacy. As you ponder your purpose in life and wonder how you fit into God's Big Plan, you will find the answers in Scripture and explained via sermons and Bible lessons. If you ask God for wisdom and insight, He promises to give individualized attention.

Call to Me, and I will answer you, and show you great and mighty things, which you do not know. (Jeremiah 33:3).

Although George Washington Carver[4] was born into slavery, he ultimately obtained a university degree in agriculture and was hired by Booker T. Washington to teach at the newly formed Tuskegee Institute in Alabama.

Eventually, Carver discovered over 300 uses for the peanut, including soups, sauces, bleach, metal polish, linoleum, axel grease, and synthetic rubber. He received many awards and became a personal advisor to several world leaders.

In 1921, Dr. Carver was testifying before a Congressional committee when the Chairman asked:

"Mr. Carver, how did you learn all of these things?"
Carver answered, "From an old book."
"What book?" asked the Senator.
Carver replied, "The Bible."
The Senator inquired, "Does the Bible tell about peanuts?"
"No, sir," Dr. Carver replied, "But it tells me about the God who made the peanut. I asked Him to show me what to do with the peanut and He did."[5]

Pray! Ask God what you want to know. *Then, stop, look and listen!* In addition to His Word, God may respond to your requests through divine inspiration and synchronicity.

Divine Inspiration

When an aggressive persecutor of Christians named Saul of Tarsus experienced a "road to Damascus moment" leading to his becoming the

Apostle Paul, there is no doubt God spoke clearly, directly, and audibly to him.[6] His conversation with Jesus that day dramatically redefined his life and altered the course of history.

God's communication with Christians today is much less dramatic and His purpose often less clear but there is no doubt He still speaks directly to individuals.

The Holy Spirit may use the divine energy of inspiration to communicate through your personal awareness. Have you ever just *known* something without any conscious reasoning or analysis? It is likely that God was giving you an assignment...a responsibility to take a particular action which you may or may not understand.

As my fiancé was completing her nursing school education in Charlotte, North Carolina, I was stationed onboard USS *Fidelity* in Charleston, South Carolina. It was not uncommon for the ship to put to sea at first light on a Monday morning and spend several days conducting training drills and exercises.

> One night during the Spring of '64, as *Fidelity* was riding-out a severe Atlantic storm, I was on duty alone in the Radio Shack. Around two o'clock in the morning, I needed to go topside and deliver a weather advisory to the OOD (Officer of the Deck).
>
> The wind and stormy sea were buffeting the ship, causing it to pitch and roll as I stepped into the darkness of the weather decks and climbed the exterior ladder to the next level.
>
> As I arrived at the Pilot House and was opening the watertight door, the ship listed heavily. *The few seconds she remained suspended in that position seemed like an eternity!* When the ship miraculously righted herself, I entered the Pilot House, grateful to safely escape the potential deadly effects of the storm.

Upon reaching port several days later, I shared my scary experience with Martha. Incredibly, she had suddenly awakened at that precise time with a strong sense that I was in harm's way. Without hesitation and without understanding why, she began praying for me.

During the time of my gravest danger, Martha was on her knees praying for me...and I absolutely believe God answered her prayer!

Perhaps your experience has less drama, but it is likely that God has similarly communicated with you. You may have felt an inclination so strong that you knew God was giving you an assignment. What was your response? Instant obedience? Procrastination?

There was an incident in my life I had chosen to not include in this book, but my Inner Coach would not let the matter drop. His incessant pressure forces me to make this confession:

It was in the Spring 1963, when Denny reported as my replacement in the Navy's Communication Center in Monterey, California.

He was a big guy, quiet and reserved. Although we worked together for a month or so, work schedules and individual lifestyles kept us from developing a close friendship. I was a single Sailor; he was a married man with a small child at home.

Until 49 years after leaving for my new assignment on the East Coast, I doubt Denny's name ever once entered my mind. One day, however, his name—including his very unusual surname—suddenly began popping into my conscious mind.

When Facebook searches for Denny turned-up empty, I began looking for someone having the same last name.

Finally, I found and contacted a person who turned out to be his daughter. Shortly thereafter, she sent me Denny's email address, which I promptly laid aside. Eventually, the promptings of my Coach diminished and were forgotten.

Here is my shameful confession:

- *Divine inspiration* brought Denny's name into my mind.
- God provided what I needed to initiate contact with him.
- Procrastinating, I never made the effort to contact him.

Later, Denny's daughter sadly advised me that he had passed away within six months of my neglecting to contact him.

I understood *too late* that God wanted to use me as a conduit to send a message to a shipmate I had hardly known nearly 50 years earlier.

Although God will never force you to do what He wants you to do, it is always best to obey immediately. Procrastinating and postponing obedience— *especially when you don't understand the "why"*—may lead to missed opportunities and to lifelong regrets.

The Mystery of Synchronicity

Have you ever found yourself thinking about someone you haven't seen or heard from in years and unexpectedly meeting that person the next day? Or hear from or about that individual not long after thinking about them?

Was it a coincidence or was it a "God thing?"

At times, God gets our attention and communicates through *synchronicity*... the simultaneous but unlikely occurrence of events which have no discernible cause but later appear to be significant.

The longer you live (and if you're paying attention!) you will become more and more aware of this fundamental truth:

A Smooth Stone
There is much more to life than what is clearly visible!

God sees your life quite differently than you perceive it. He sees your life as a beautiful tapestry woven with invisible threads. Over time, these threads connect with people and events to create the totality of your life.

The invisible threads of life sometimes encounter unanticipated connection points and form what we call a "coincidence." Squire Rushnell[7] developed a hypothesis called *God Winks* which posits that a coincidence is sometimes so astonishing it could come only from a divine source. In that context, God may ordain a divine appointment in your life that appears as a coincidence.

Over time, you may realize that God gives precursors of His plan for your life by inserting clues into common, everyday events. Through the lens of 20/20 hindsight, you may discover clues He cleverly but clearly placed in your life.

> As a happy-go-lucky 16-year-old on a summer afternoon in 1957, a friend and I hitched a ride to Mint Hill to spend time with our girlfriends. Around 10 p.m. on that brightly moonlit night, we began the 15-mile hike to my home in the Dilworth section of Charlotte.

> I vividly recall strolling down Lawyers Road and noticing a little white house situated on a hill to my left, just up the road from McAlpine Creek.

> Six years later, as the funeral procession for my father was en route to the cemetery in Mint Hill, my older brother and I commented on the installation process of a mobile home just past McAlpine Creek, next door to a little white house situated on a hill.

Several weeks after the funeral, my buddy and I went on a double date with two student nurses. Somehow, I was more attracted to *his* date than mine and wanted to learn everything I could about her! Shortly thereafter, she (Martha) and I were a steady couple.

Two weeks later, it was déjà vu for me as I went to meet her parents for the first time. We drove down the hill on Lawyers Road, crossed the McAlpine Creek bridge, and turned into the driveway of a little white house situated on a hill...right next door to a newly installed mobile home!

God indeed works in mysterious ways! If you are paying attention, you may recognize God Winks in your life. God always has a purpose for winking a coincidence into your life. Sometimes, He wants to use you to be a blessing to someone else. Sometimes, it's the other way around...He wants you to receive the blessing!

Accept Your Role

John Wooden's role as UCLA's head basketball coach was to understand and plan the best possible future for his players. Each player's role was to accept and respect his role and to obey his leadership.

When you accepted Jesus as your personal Savior, your Inner Coach moved in to nurture and guide you toward your best future. Your role is to accept and respect the Coach's role and to studiously obey His leadership.

Most of your life will be routine and mundane but once in a while, you will *know* He wants you to step outside your comfort zone. Be assured that if you willingly obey and follow His leadership, He will equip you with everything necessary for your success.

Here is the way Mother Teresa is said to have described obedience in accepting her role in God's Big Plan:

I am a little pencil in God's hands. He does the thinking. He does the writing. He does everything and sometimes it is really hard because it is a broken pencil and He has to sharpen it a little more.

When obedience requires mental toughness, courage, and strength beyond your normal capability, be assured that your Coach will always provide special powers, as necessary.

Chapter Notes

1. Samuel Taylor Coleridge (1772–1834) was an English poet, philosopher, and theologian.

2. George Smith Patton Jr. (1885–1945) was a general of the United States Army who commanded the United States Third Army in France and Germany after the Allied invasion of Normandy in June 1944.

3. Source: An article titled *The True Story of the Patton Prayer* by Msgr. James H. O'Neill printed as a government document in 1950. A reference copy was obtained from www.pattonhq.com on February 17, 2020.

4. George Washington Carver (1864–1943) was an African American scientist and educator.

5. Charles E. Jones, *The Books You Read*, Harrisburg, PA: Executive Books, 1985, p132.

6. See Acts 9:1-7.

7. Squire Rushnell (b. 1938) is an American author and inspirational speaker who coined the term *God Winks*. His book *Divine Alignment* and the books in his *God Winks* series are highly recommended.

Chapter 7
The Power to Prevail

We must leave our mark on our life while we have it in our power.
—Isak Dinesen[1]

The now-famous equation "knowledge is power" was coined by Francis Bacon[2] in 1597. Although its context is uncertain, its literal meaning has become a cliché over the past several centuries.

In any context, the value of knowledge cannot be disputed. However, in and of itself, knowledge is actually potential power. Until applied to a specific purpose, the intrinsic power of knowledge remains dormant. For example, you can learn "how to" swim by reading a book but you cannot become an Olympic swimmer until water is added.

A Smooth Stone
The acquisition plus the application of knowledge is power!

Albert Einstein's[3] in-depth knowledge of physics was documented as the theory of relativity and published in 1905 and 1916. Many years later, scientists used this knowledge to develop the nuclear reactor and in 1945, to deliver the first atomic bomb. The real power in Einstein's knowledge came with the application of his knowledge...and the world was forever changed!

The War vs. the Word

Shortly after a beautiful sunrise over Honolulu on Sunday, December 7, 1941, an intense cover of black smoke darkened the skies. Just before 8 a.m., hundreds of Japanese bombers and fighter planes led by Lt. Matsuo Fuchida began bombing and strafing the naval base at Pearl Harbor.

More than 2,400 Americans died in this devastating surprise attack; many more were wounded. Nearly 20 United States Navy vessels, including eight battleships and over 300 airplanes were destroyed or severely damaged.

This event instigated by Lt. Fuchida's actions ignited World War II in the Pacific. Over the next 1,338 days, 111,606 Americans were killed or listed as missing. During the same period, 1,740,000 Japanese military personnel plus 393,400 civilians lost their lives.[4]

On August 6, 1945, the American B29 bomber *Enola Gay* dropped a five-ton bomb over the Japanese city of Hiroshima. An atomic blast equivalent to the power of 15,000 tons of TNT reduced four square miles of the city to rubble. Two days later, a similar bomb was released over Nagasaki.

The actual loss of life due to these horrific blasts will never be known but the estimates of those killed or wounded in Hiroshima (150,000) and Nagasaki (75,000) are considered conservative.

The immense destruction and carnage occurring in Japan over three days in August 1945 provides the single-most graphic example of power ever released via the *application* of knowledge.

Unknown to anyone during the entire war, God was preparing to use an obscure American prisoner of war and the *application* of His Word to radically change Matsuo Fuchida's life.

Jake DeShazer was repeatedly tortured by his Japanese captors and kept in solitary confinement during 40 months of captivity. As hatred for the Japanese festered within him, Jake was miraculously allowed to have access to a Bible. With possession of the Bible for just three weeks, he recognized its message as the reason for his survival and resolved to become a devout Christian.

His conversion led to a desire to learn a few words of the Japanese language and begin treating his captors with respect. Jake was amazed that this new attitude impressed one of the guards causing him to respond similarly!

At war's end, Jake DeShazer returned home, entered Seattle Pacific College, and began studying to be a missionary. He and his wife arrived in Japan as Methodist missionaries in December 1948.

Mitsuo Fuchida became a Christian after reading a tract written by DeShazer titled, *I Was a Prisoner of Japan* and met him in June 1950. Fuchida committed the remainder of his life to traveling the world, sharing his Christian testimony.[5]

The *physical* power of knowledge unleashed by scientists resulted in destruction and eternal misery. Most likely, the personal influence and legacy of those who perished in Hiroshima and Nagasaki diminished to near zero.

The *spiritual* power released through Jake DeShazer's application of God's Word created a new life and a new legacy for thousands of people worldwide. The ripple effect of his obedience continues throughout the world today... more than 70 years after the process began.

The improbability of these events unfolding during the atrocities of war is astounding. It can only be attributed to the power of God's Word manifested through the life of one brand-new Christian!

The Bible — More Than Words

The First World War (1914–1918) was idealistically described as "the war to end all wars." but nations have yet to work successfully to that end. Not unlike the conflict between nations, Christians are daily engaged in a never-ending war with a very formidable enemy.

> Stay alert! Watch out for your great enemy, the devil. He prowls around like a roaring lion, looking for someone to devour. (1 Peter 5:8, NLT).

The Devil's *modus operandi* is to place seemingly irresistible temptations and roadblocks squarely on the path of your life. His purpose is to rob you of the joy and blessings of living a Christ-centered life and to diminish your Christian influence.

The only viable defense against the wiles of the Devil is the personal application of the life-changing, supernatural power of God's written Word.

> The word of God is *living* and *powerful* and sharper than any two-edged

sword, piercing even to the division of soul and spirit, and of joints and marrow, and is a discerner of the thoughts and intents of the heart. (Hebrews 4:12, emphasis added).

God's Word has the power to guide you into a lifestyle consistent with a life worth following. The truth of the Bible can unshackle any detrimental habits and free you to develop more positive patterns of behavior.

Several thousand years ago, an unknown psalmist—probably David or Ezra—sensed a need for a more powerful, closer relationship with God. Recognizing the contrast between God's holiness and his own sinful nature, he chose this proactive defense against life's inescapable uncertainties:

Your word I have hidden in my heart that I might not sin against You. (Psalm 119:11).

In essence, the psalmist's stated commitment to God was, "I know the future will inevitably bring me face-to-face with temptations that seem irresistible. Therefore, I am preparing for the future by storing the power of Your Word in the arsenal of my memory bank."

A Smooth Stone
When the time of need arrives, the time for preparation has passed.

You may occasionally feel powerless and uneasy without understanding the reason. God may see your attitude toward His Word becoming casual and inconsistent and be gently nudging you to tighten-up your relationship with Him. You can move closer to Him by following the psalmist's centuries-old strategy. It is still as simple as ABC:

A. Read the Bible regularly.
B. Ask God to reveal its relevance to you.
C. Memorize at least one verse *every* week.

The final chapter of this book is a 52-week *Gratitude Journal* designed to focus on your blessings and assist you in memorizing Scripture. As the Word of God courses through your mind, a habit will develop to filter your thoughts and encourage righteous living.

KEY POINT: The more time you spend reading and meditating on the written Word of God, the more intimate your relationship with the *living* Word —Jesus —will become.

The Holy Spirit is ready to activate the ultimate weapon necessary for a victorious Christian life. He will bring the Bible's message to life in your heart and use its power to transform your life...*if you let Him!*

The choice is yours. *Not to decide is to decide.*

The Mysterious Power of Faith

Life is filled with mystery. Intuition is a mystery. How the brain becomes the mind is a mystery. How the body heals itself is a mystery. Electricity and personal faith are mysteries.

The mystery of electricity has much in common with the mystery of faith. A woman once approached the great inventor Thomas Edison with this question: "Mr. Edison, what is electricity?" He replied, "Madam, electricity is. Use it."

Rather than struggling to precisely define faith, you will be well served to accept that faith simply "is" and maximize its power to live a life worthy of emulation and well-pleasing to the Lord.

Faith is not a science experiment to be tested and understood in a laboratory but is an intriguing mystery to be personally experienced.

The key to unlocking the legacy of a life worth following is making the choice to exercise faith—even with trepidation—in the absolute infinite power of God. It is believing that God is who He said He is and will do what He said He will do.

Spiritual faith is the supernatural power that establishes an instantaneous, never-ending relationship between a non-believer and the eternal God. The

Apostle Paul clearly explained the linkage between salvation and faith by defining the process[6] by which personal faith is obtained:

- For "Everyone who calls on the name of the Lord will be saved." But how can they call on him to save them unless they believe in him? And how can they believe in him if they have never heard about him? And how can they hear about him unless someone tells them?

- So, faith comes from hearing, that is, hearing the Good News about Christ.

- For it is by believing in your heart that you are made right with God, and it is by openly declaring your faith that you are saved.

There are times when your faith will be tested. When it falters, do what the apostles and other believers through the ages have done, seek encouragement in God's Word.

So be truly glad. There is wonderful joy ahead, even though you must endure many trials for a little while. These trials will show that your faith is genuine. It is being tested as fire tests and purifies gold—though your faith is far more precious than mere gold. So, when your faith remains strong through many trials, it will bring you much praise and glory and honor on the day when Jesus Christ is revealed to the whole world. (1 Peter 1:6-7, NLT).

A Smooth Stone
Faith does not make things easy; it makes them possible.

Look to God for courage and strength. Your faith will be strengthened each time you send up an urgent little prayer, take a deep breath, and obey His will. Remember, God will *always* honor your faith by providing the courage, wisdom, and power to do what He asks you to do.

How strong is your faith right now? Compare its strength to the power of electricity. Does your faith have low wattage "night-light" power or megawatt "stadium lighting" power? Think about it.

Belief: A Life-Changing Power

What you *know* that you *know* is what you believe.

Unfortunately, some of what you believe is inconsistent with truth and reality. Will Rogers[7] is said to have opined, "It isn't what we *don't know* that gives us trouble, it's what we do *know* that ain't so."

A number of years ago, fifteen leading university and college professors met to develop a brief statement to define the art of moving human beings to action. After many hours of give-and-take discussion, the group settled on this description:

> *What the mind attends to, it considers: what it does not attend to, it dismisses. What the mind attends to continually, it believes. And, what the mind believes it eventually does!*[8]

Right or wrong—true or untrue—what you believe determines your behavior. Unambiguous, non-negotiable personal beliefs activate miraculous powers within the subconscious mind that result in behavior patterns—habits—that mold and shape your life.

Strong beliefs definitively prescribe the quality and effectiveness of your life and perhaps, its length. The unalterable pattern is:

a. Your beliefs dictate your behavior.
b. Your behavior determines your destiny.
c. Your destiny reveals your legacy.

A Smooth Stone
What I believe determines what I become.

There appear to be two fundamental types of belief. All data entering the brain seems to be analyzed and rejected outright or flagged as either an *intellectual* belief or a *core* belief:

1. *Intellectual beliefs* tend to be superficial. We consider them to be true but, "So what?" For example, I believe cows would live longer if they weren't made out of steaks and leather.

2. *Core beliefs* are foundational values that form the very essence of our being and define who we *really* are.

The Belief System residing in the sub-conscious mind has tirelessly accumulated, categorized, and prioritized information and opinions since the earliest days of childhood. As a biased arbiter, it decides our responses to optional personal behavior and interactions.

What you believe directly influences the quality and effectiveness of your life and provides the baselines for success in the Game of Life. Napoleon Hill[9] famously observed, "Whatever the mind can conceive and believe, the mind can achieve."

The strength of specific beliefs dramatically expands as your subconscious is peppered with constant affirmations. Your Belief System is judgment-free on incoming affirmations but recognizes consistency. For example, a Christian rarely praying or reading the Bible instructs the Belief System to place minimum value on these activities.

Conversely, a Christian whose daily routine includes prayer and meditation on Scriptural principles sends a powerful, value-laden message to the subconscious. The power of affirmations generated by living a godly lifestyle dramatically affects your Belief System.

A conscious decision to proactively expand your Belief System via frequent affirmations of optimism and positivity is a wise one. One actionable game plan is to create a written *I Believe* list. Frequently reviewing and updating your list will authorize your subconscious mind to revise your Belief System accordingly.

These *I Believe* affirmations illustrate the process:

I believe that what I *believe* determines what I *become*.
I believe only Jesus can control my life without screwing it up.
I believe what I *am* is more important than what I *do*.
I believe thoughts have consequences.
I believe life begins at conception and never ends.
I believe Heaven is a real, physical place.
I believe Christians move into Heaven at the instant of death.
I believe I am who God says I am.
I believe kindness never goes unrewarded.
I believe adversity always precedes achievement.
I believe I can do everything the Bible says I can do.
I believe change is inevitable, but growth is optional.
I believe today's decisions dramatically affect my destiny.

Your Belief System is the gateway to powers beyond your imagination!
It is a dynamic reservoir of wisdom, courage, and tenacity for living a life worth following and developing a lasting legacy.

What's in a Name?

More than 400 years ago, Shakespeare's main character in *Romeo and Juliet* forlornly asked his beloved, "What's in a name?" The essence of his question was, "What *difference* does a name make?" Today, every person's character and influence determine their "difference" and tips the scale to somewhere between *not much* and *immeasurable*.

Orphaned at an early age and cast-off by an uncaring uncle, Billy Batson[10] was living on the streets of New York City in 1940. He sold newspapers by day and scrounged for food and lodging at night. During a surprise encounter one evening with a man having a powerful name, Billy was endowed with supernatural powers. Ever after, as he shouted the man's name—*Shazam!*—Billy received the wisdom of Solomon, the strength of Hercules, the stamina of Atlas, the power of Zeus, the courage of Achilles, and the speed of Mercury.

The powerful name of Shazam and its associated transforming power is obviously fictional but even *if* true, its power would pale in comparison with the matchless name of Jesus!

Jesus! Jesus! Jesus! There *is* something about that name!

> Therefore God also has highly exalted Him and given Him the name which is above every name, that at the name of Jesus *every* knee should bow, of those in heaven, and of those on earth, and of those under the earth, and that every tongue should confess that Jesus Christ is Lord, to the glory of God the Father. (Philippians 2:9-11, emphasis added).

The unspeakable power in the name of Jesus will be categorically demonstrated at a future time known only to God. In an instant, every soul ever born on Earth—estimated to be 108 billion people as of 2019[11]—will humbly and worshipfully bow and acknowledge the deity of Jesus Christ.

In the interim, non-believers have God's assurance of hope for them in the future.

> If you openly declare that Jesus is Lord and believe in your heart that God raised him from the dead *you will be saved*. (Romans 10:9 NLT, emphasis added).

Meanwhile, Christians have here-and-now access to absolute security and confidence for daily living through the power in the name of Jesus.

> The name of the Lord is a strong fortress, the godly run to him and are safe. (Proverbs 18:10, NLT).

> I can do all things through Christ who strengthens me. (Philippians 4:13).

God explicitly defined the standard that Christians must meet to live with a sense of security and achieve success via the power in the name of Jesus:

And whatever you do in word or deed, do all in the name of the Lord Jesus, giving thanks to God the Father through Him. (Colossians 3:17).

Stressing this truly relevant point, Adrian Rogers[12] said, "To live in the Spirit and to do everything in the name of Jesus means that we will do nothing to dishonor His name."

Before making any significant decision, always ask, "Would Jesus give His endorsement by signing His name to my decision?" Unless you are confident of His approval, you should reevaluate your reasons and rationale for the decision.

Each unique power described in this chapter is available to everyone, but its super-octane potential is available only to Christians. Each is capable of working independently or synergistically but common focus is required to generate the life-changing effects necessary for a life worth following.

Chapter Notes

1. Isak Dinesen (1885–1962) was a pseudonym of the Danish writer, Karen Christence Dinesen. Perhaps her best-known work is *Out of Africa*, a memoir of her years in Kenya.

2. Sir Francis Bacon (1561–1626) was an English philosopher, lawyer, statesman, and author; a leading figure in natural philosophy and in the field of scientific methodology.

3. Albert Einstein (1879–1955) was a German mathematician and physicist who developed the special and general theories of relativity. He was awarded the Nobel Prize for physics in 1921. After being targeted by the German Nazi Party, Einstein emigrated to the United States in 1933 and became a citizen in 1940. Source: www.biography.com

4. Source: http://www.pwencycl.kgbudge.com/C/a/Casualties.htm

5. The amazing true story of Matsuo Fuchida, Jake DeShazer and the events

of WWII in the Pacific are detailed in the highly recommended book, *Wounded Tiger* by T Martin Bennett, Brown Books Publishing Group, Dallas, TX, www.BrownBooks.com

6. Romans 10:13-14, Romans 10:17 and Romans 10:10, NLT.

7. Will Rogers (1879–1935) was an American actor, cowboy, humorist, newspaper columnist and social commentator known for his dry but direct wit.

8. Source: *Live a New Life* by David Guy Powers, 1948, Doubleday & Co., Inc., Garden City, NY, p. 90.

9. Napoleon Hill (1883–1970) was an American self-help author best known for his book *Think and Grow Rich* which is among the ten bestselling self-help books of all time.

10. Billy Batson is a fictional comic book character created by artist C. C. Beck and writer Bill Parker in 1939. Billy's alter-ego, *Captain Marvel,* first appeared in Whiz Comics #2 (cover-dated February 1940), published by Fawcett Comics. Source: www.dcuniverse.com

11. The Population Reference Bureau (PRB) estimates the current world population as approximately 7.5 billion. PRB estimates that as of 2019, more than 108 billion people have been born on Earth and that by 2050, about 113 billion people will have lived on the planet. Source: https://www.prb.org/howmanypeoplehaveeverlivedonearth/

12. Adrian Rogers (1931–2005) was pastor of Bellevue Baptist Church (Memphis, Tennessee) for 33 years and served three terms as president of the Southern Baptist Convention.

Chapter 8
The Power Within

What lies behind us and what lies ahead of us
are tiny matters compared to what lives within us.
—Henry David Thoreau[1]

The sun dawned bright and early in San Diego on Saturday, February 8, 1958. Several hours earlier, I had been delivered like a new-born babe into a strange and unfamiliar new world...the United States Navy.

My Navy adventure began when a herd of 74 other bewildered recruits from varying parts of the country joined me to form Recruit Company 106. Although different sizes, shapes, colors, and personalities, we became very much alike. We were stripped of *everything* and given the same haircut and the same clothes—skivvies, flat pocket denim dungarees, chambray shirts, a pair of boondockers, white hats—and a ditty bag.

The ditty bag provided everything necessary—except grit and fortitude— to make it through Boot Camp. It contained toiletry items, clothes stops,[2] a sewing kit, shoe polish, and a copy of *The Bluejackets Manual*—the Navy's handbook of process and procedures.

After nine weeks of training and indoctrination, we took our ditty bag and left boot camp. Decked-out in dress blues with thirteen-button bell-bottom trousers, spit-shined shoes, and topped off with the enlisted man's famous Dixie Cup white hat, we were immediately recognizable as a United States Navy Sailor.

Distinct Similarities

Are you immediately recognizable as a Christian?

Your attitude and observable behavior determine the way you are perceived by others. Every Navy recruit learns "there is a right way, a wrong way, and the

Navy way of doing things" and receives a *Bluejackets Manual* for guidance in decision making.

Christians learn that the options offered at critical decision points must be carefully evaluated. The Bible clearly explains that some options *appear* to be "right" but will be exposed as a *wrong* way when misleading assertions are brushed aside.

> There is a way that seems right to a man, but its end is the way of death. (Proverbs 14:12).

A Smooth Stone
When in doubt, don't!

You need direct access to wisdom to choose and follow the right way consistently. The immutable truth is that Jesus Christ *is* wisdom and the *only* right way:

> Christ is the power of God and the wisdom of God. (1 Corinthians 1:24b, NLT).

> Jesus answered, "I am the *way* and the truth and the life. No one comes to the Father except through me." (John 14:6, NIV, emphasis added).

Just as a Navy recruit's new apparel differentiates a new life from a former life, the evidence of your Inner Coach's influence on your behavior identifies the "new" you:

> For you are all children of God through faith in Christ Jesus. And all who have been united with Christ in baptism have put on Christ, like putting on new clothes. (Galatians 3:26-27, NLT).

> I am overwhelmed with joy in the LORD my God! For he has dressed me with the clothing of salvation and draped me in a robe of righteousness. (Isaiah 61:10a, NLT).

Military expectations dictate that Sailors exhibit lifestyles and behaviors that honor the USA and the Navy. Similarly, God has definitive expectations for a Christian's lifestyle and behavior. The perception others have of you is a major factor in your ability to achieve a life worth following.

There is little commonality between the way we see ourselves, the way others see us, and the way God sees us. It is like He and we are looking at different people.

We can only see ourselves from the perspective of our past experience flavored by what we currently know and rationalize about ourselves. Other people merge their *opinion* with their *perception* of your actions to conclude what they *think* you are.

Fortunately, Scripture clearly teaches that God sees Christians as being "in Christ."

> Therefore, if anyone is in Christ, he is a new creation; old things have passed away; behold, all things have become new. (2 Corinthians 5:17).

My layman's understanding of being in Christ is that when God views a Christian, He sees Christ's righteousness! He has chosen to see us as we *will be* in the future.

Let's put this in perspective...compared to Christ, you are essentially an unkempt bum with unsavory behavior and a despicable past. But when God views you through the prism of Jesus' blood, shed on the cross, He sees a righteous and pure life. *Amazing! Praise the Lord!*

The Invisible Ditty Bag

What is essential is invisible to the eye.[3]

The continuing process for crafting a life worth emulating and creating a lasting legacy has two primary components: the visible and the invisible. Interestingly, the basis of everything—from human beings to iPads—within the visible component is 100% comprised of *invisible* elements. The invisible world provides the intelligence and energizing source for every success you achieve in life.

During one magical moment in history, you were delivered as a new-born babe into the strange and unfamiliar new world of life! You arrived equipped with an invisible ditty bag containing everything—except faith and obedience— necessary to live a long and effective Christian life.

Your only remaining need was an Inner Coach to provide guidance through the morass of life. When you accepted Jesus Christ as your personal Savior, the Holy Spirit took up residence in your heart to provide 24/7 encouragement and guidance for implementing God's plan for your life.

The gap between where you *are* and where you *want to be* in life can be bridged by connecting the invisible interlocking pieces of your life puzzle. The integral pieces for achieving your life's mission resides in the ditty bag of your being. Your Inner Coach will identify, integrate and activate subsets of these attributes to produce amazing results.

Your ditty bag is filled with innumerable invisible, yet positive attitudes and assets including:

> Appreciation, character, cheerfulness, compassion, confidence, contentment, courage, empathy, encouragement, enthusiasm, forgiveness, friendliness, gentleness, goodness, grace, gratitude, honesty, hope, humility, influence, integrity, intuition, joy, love, patience, pleasantness, prudence, satisfaction, selflessness, sincerity, supportiveness, sympathy, thoughtfulness, trustworthiness and truthfulness.

A Smooth Stone
Invest your invisible assets wisely.

Since so much is unknown and unseeable, sensing a need to make changes in your lifestyle will likely cause apprehension and perhaps, a modicum of doubt. Your responsibility is to have faith and believe—whatever your past or your present—that your life can be refurbished to become a more significant part of God's Big Plan.

You must agree to actively obey and work with your Inner Coach to live a godlier life. It is an intimidating thought but God has promised that you can muster-up the desire, courage, strength, and resources to do your part.

> His divine power has given to us *all* things that pertain to life and godliness. (2 Peter 1:3, emphasis added).

Additionally, the Apostle Paul was inspired to remind us that we can do *nothing* without Jesus but *with* Him, *nothing* is impossible.

> I can do all things through Christ who strengthens me. (Philippians 4:13).

Not unlike the way God viewed Paul, He sees you as a unique conduit of His love. When your ditty bag assets link to His supernatural powers, something good is gonna happen!

Connecting the Invisibles

God designed love as the *preeminent* power for the express purpose of linking individual components of His creation to each other, to Himself and at the discretion of your Inner Coach, to circumstances and opportunities.

Christians often make the mistake of thinking God loves us the way we love baseball, apple pie, and each other. *Wrong!* God's love is vastly different from human love. His love is unconditional and is not based on feelings, emotions or personality.

While God loves everyone, He places a protective banner of love over those who love Jesus. Furthermore, the Bible proclaims that God is love!

> Whoever does not love does not know God, because God is love. (1 John 4:8, NIV).

Since He never changes and cannot lie,[4] we know that God's love for us is independent of our attitudes and behavior. Our finite mind simply cannot comprehend the fact that He knows every grimy detail of every thought and behavior we've experienced...and loves us anyway!

So, what does this knowledge of God's love have to do with living a life worth following? The short answer is, "*Everything!*" When asked his belief on the meaning of love, Martin Luther King Jr. wrote:

> Love is the greatest force in the universe. It is the heartbeat of the moral cosmos. He who loves is a participant in the being of God.[5]

You are a participant in the being of God! What an awesome blessing! Isn't it reassuring to know that Scripture affirms this American icon's insight?

> For God wanted them to know that the riches and glory of Christ are for you Gentiles, too. And this is the secret: *Christ lives in you.* This gives you assurance of sharing his glory. (Colossians 1:27, NLT, emphasis added).

Another wonderful blessing is the assurance that being *in Christ,* you don't have to go through life burdened by past indiscretions, sins, and disappointments. Your "old" life was figuratively crucified with Christ and your present life is infused with the life and power of Christ.

> My old self has been crucified with Christ. It is no longer I who live, but Christ lives in me. So I live in this earthly body by trusting in the Son of God, who loved me and gave himself for me. (Galatians 2:20, NLT).

> But you belong to God, my dear children. You have already won a victory over those people, because the Spirit who lives in you is greater than the spirit who lives in the world. (1 John 4:4, NLT).

The *omnipotent* power of love and the matchless name of Jesus are the dynamics that activate the power in God's Word to release the ancillary powers of knowledge, faith, and belief.

Our Common Condition

We have an invisible enemy opposed to God and all that is good. This adversary relentlessly wages war against our desire to live a life worth emulating.

The Devil hates God! He hates love because God is love. He hates you because you love Jesus. Your only defense against this antagonist is maintaining a close relationship with God. Every inch you cede to the Devil by giving-in to his temptations will be used to diminish the power of God's love in your life.

A Smooth Stone
You determine the closeness of your relationship with God.

An old-time hymn captures the essence of our common weakness. There's a line in the hymn's lyrics that should grab our attention and force some self-reflection: "Prone to wander, Lord, I feel it. Prone to leave the God I love."[6]

In our heart of hearts, we do not want to wander from a close relationship with God but human weakness, habits and the distractions of life tend to separate us from Him and His Word.

The Apostle Paul described his weakness—and ours—when he wrote, "I want to do what is good, but I don't. I don't want to do what is wrong, but I do it anyway."[7]

King David was evidently struggling with the same problem when he composed this prayer:

> With my whole heart I have sought You; Oh, let me not wander from Your commandments! (Psalm 119:10).

Activate the Power

An active love for Jesus and a desire to know Him better are the essential ingredients for powering-up a life worth emulating. The depth of your love dictates the time and effort you invest in developing your relationship with Jesus.

A Smooth Stone
You are as close to Jesus as you want to be!

Cultivating a deeper relationship with Jesus requires *knowing* and *obeying* Him. He is so straightforward in communicating His expectations that there is little room for misunderstanding:

If you love me, obey my commandments. (John 14:15, NLT).

Whoever has my commands and keeps them is the one who loves me. The one who loves me will be loved by my Father, and I too will love them and show myself to them. (John 14:21, NIV).

Anyone who loves me will obey my teaching. My Father will love them, and we will come to them and make our home with them. (John 14:23, NIV).

By stipulating 100% obedience, Jesus infers that you and I are responsible for seeking to know His commandments. It is important to remember that His teachings are *commandments*, not simply suggestions, really good ideas or recommendations.

This specific commandment has far-reaching implications and can jump-start your quest to realign your life to one worth emulating:

A new command I give you: Love one another. As I have loved you, so you must love one another. By this everyone will know that you are my disciples, if you love one another. (John 13:34-35, NIV).

We often take many of life's essentials, e.g. love for granted and consider the routine of life as insignificant. That is a mistake...little things mean a lot!

Chapter Notes

1. Henry David Thoreau (1817–1862) was an American essayist, poet, and philosopher best known for his book *Walden*—a reflection upon simple living—and his essay *Civil Disobedience*, an argument for disobedience to an unjust state.

2. A clothes stop was a short small diameter cord with metal ends to keep the cord from fraying and was used to tie a recruit's hand-scrubbed clothing to a clothesline for drying. The Navy stopped issuing clothes stops to recruits in 1973.

3. Antoine de Saint-Exupéry (1900–1944) was a French writer, poet, aristocrat, journalist and pioneering aviator. This quote is from his book *The Little Prince* originally published in 1943.

4. God is perfect and therefore, cannot lie. Scripture proclaims, "In hope of eternal life, which God, *who cannot lie,* promised before time began." (Titus 1:2, emphasis added).

5. Martin Luther King, Jr. (1929–1968) was an American minister and activist and the most visible leader in the Civil Rights Movement from 1955 until his assassination in 1968. According to www.cnn.com (February 12, 2020), a 1960's handwritten note believed to be a response to someone asking his belief about the meaning of love has been found.

6. The hymn *Come Thou Fount of Every Blessing* was written in 1757 by Robert Robinson (1735–1790), an English minister.

7. Romans 7:19, NLT.

Chapter 9
The Law of Little Things

I am a little pencil in God's hands.
—Mother Teresa

The world's philosophy says that bigger is better and smaller is not as good; that more is better and less is lousy. Common belief teaches there is strength in numbers and lesser numbers suggest weakness.

The truth is that bigger or smaller, more or less in number, strong or weak is not the issue. The issue always is whether or not God is actively involved in your thoughts, plans, and behavior.

History records many instances of God using insignificant people and small things to achieve significant results:

- A farmer named Shamgar[1] used an everyday farm tool to singlehandedly kill 600 of Israel's enemies.

- Greek philosophers believed the atom was the smallest thing in the universe and could not be divided. Subsequently, our Creator allowed mankind to learn much more about this minuscule bit of matter, including the wherewithal to split it to develop atomic and nuclear power.

God chose—sometimes, it seems with humor—to permit people like you and me to accomplish things we could never imagine. Scripture describes His modus operandi:

God has chosen the foolish things of the world to put to shame the wise, and God has chosen the weak things of the world to put to shame the things which are mighty (1 Corinthians 1:27).

Many believers were not born into a wealthy, influential family and are neither wise nor powerful in human terms. Fortunately, God does not require brilliance or a powerful influence for a person to become a Christian.

Only those who accept the strength and wisdom of His outpouring of love on the cross at Calvary can receive and believe the gospel. Many non-believers view the gospel as a foolish message believed by weaklings needing a crutch to get through life.

Let's face it...life is sometimes tough but is mostly uneventful. Everyday aggravations sprinkled among occasional victories coalesce to update your personal past.

Your *past* is continually modified to include the effects of your decisions—both large and small. God can use your seemingly insignificant words and deeds to dynamically and eternally change the lives of other people.

A Smooth Stone
Little things don't mean a lot... little things mean everything!

The Butterfly Effect

Does your life sometimes seem chaotic? Do you anticipate a future based on random events having no apparent connectivity to anything meaningful or worthwhile? *Congratulations... you are normal!*

Now, step back and remember that God sees the end from the beginning, and He has a plan—of which you are a key player—that will pull all the pieces together for a perfect ending.

> And we *know* that all things work together for good to those who love God, to those who are the called according to His purpose. (Romans 8:28, emphasis added).

In God's Plan, the most remote and seemingly random occurrence has an underlying and meaningful purpose that contributes to your legacy. This historical example graphically illustrates the critical importance of "little" things in life.

One day in the winter of 1961, Edward Lorentz[2] wanted to rerun a particular sequence of data in his lab at the Massachusetts Institute of Technology. Looking to save time, he took the shortcut of typing numbers straight from the earlier printout to restart the program.

As the computing process began, he walked down the hall for a cup of coffee. Returning an hour later, Lorenz found a totally unexpected result. The computer had simulated about two months of weather pattern forecasts but all resemblance to the original output had disappeared.

Upon reviewing the dissemblance, Lorenz concluded, "That was enough to tell me what had happened: the numbers I had typed in were not the exact original numbers but were the rounded-off values that had appeared in the original printout."

During the reboot process, Lorenz had entered 0.506 from the printout rather than its full precision value, 0.506127. The program's round-off protocol for printouts became a culprit by producing and amplifying errors until the forecast was hopelessly corrupt.

Lorenz had assumed a small numerical variation was similar to a small puff of wind, existing but unlikely to significantly impact large-scale features of the weather. However, his "shortcut" decision led to the unintentional discovery that small changes in initial conditions would produce significantly large long-term effects.

Seeking to graphically communicate the dramatic effect of small things, Lorenz shared this metaphorical description, "The nonlinear equations that govern weather have such an incredible sensitivity to initial conditions, that a butterfly flapping its wings in Brazil several weeks ago could set off a tornado in Texas."

In essence, Lorenz's theory suggests that the flap of a butterfly's wings creates a puff of air that sets air molecules into motion that motivate additional air molecules to move other air molecules, ad infinitum, until weather patterns on the other side of the planet are influenced.

How does the *Butterfly Effect* affect your life? Very simply, it illustrates the unanticipated and far-reaching effects of small decisions. Each decision leads to actions producing results or consequences that can ripple throughout future generations. The aftereffect of your decisions may positively or negatively influence the lives of people you may never know.

We need not know how our words and deeds influence others to accomplish God's Big Plan. In fact, such knowledge is beyond our comprehension.

> As you do not know the path of the wind, or how the body is formed in a mother's womb, so you cannot understand the work of God, the Maker of all things (Ecclesiastes 11:5, NIV).

The Law of the Harvest

Today is the father of tomorrow. What you are today is the sum of your every thought, decision, and behavior since the instant a doctor smacked your fanny and you screamed enthusiastically into the world.

The *Law of the Harvest* ensures that predictable outcomes—positive or negative—result from your decisions. Wise decisions spawn good outcomes; unwise choices tend toward undesirable consequences.

A major factor in unlocking a legacy that pleases God and blesses others is accepting the fact that you are responsible for *you*...and your legacy!

A Smooth Stone
The me of today makes choices; the future me lives with consequences.

The *Law of the Harvest* is an unalterable, irrevocable law that affects everyone—Christians and non-Christians alike. Its foundational principle applies to every area of life, e.g. the personal, family, friendship, financial and spiritual elements.

In order to minimize confusion or misunderstanding and to ensure its message would never change, God included this law in Scripture:

Do not be deceived, God is not mocked; for whatever a man sows, that he will also reap (Galatians 6:7).

Every farmer fully understands that (1) we reap *what* we sow, (2) we reap *more than* we sow, and (3) we reap *later* than we sow.

We reap what we sow

The law guaranteeing that we reap *what* we sow is incredibly good news for those sowing seeds from packets of good habits, e.g. gratitude, kindness, thoughtfulness, respect for others, and obedience to God. We must intentionally sow the proper seeds to reap the desired harvest.

The certainty of this principle produces a frightening thought when seeds are sown in ungodly activities or from a spirit of pride, arrogance, and self-centeredness.

> My experience shows that those who plant trouble and cultivate evil will harvest the same (Job 4:8, NLT).

Ironically, God's Word teaches that neglecting to sow *any* seed can produce an undesirable harvest.

> Remember, it is sin to know what you ought to do and then not do it (James 4:17, NLT).

We reap more than we sow

Based on experience, the farmer places seeds in the ground knowing the harvest produced will be much greater than the seeds sown. A single seed will sprout with dozens or hundreds more of the same seeds.

When I needed a PowerPoint graphic to illustrate this principle, I asked a professional horticulturist, "If one black-eyed pea is planted, how many peas can I expect to harvest?"

The informative response: "When planted properly, i.e. 42 pounds of seed planted on rows with 20" row spacing over one acre, one seed would produce 38 peas."[3]

If each of those 38 peas were planted and yielded an average crop, the harvest would be 1,444 new peas. If each of those peas then yielded an average crop when planted, the progeny of the initial pea would be 54,872. Amazingly, just ten plantings of the initial pea and its "offspring" would produce a harvest of 6,278,211,847,988,220 peas! *That is more than six quadrillion peas from planting one little seed!*

God placed infinite power in the pea but the power potential within you is exponentially greater! The amazing power in a pea is restricted to a single function—producing more peas. The power He placed within you is *unlimited and unrestricted!*

You have been given the responsibility to manage and maximize your innate power by planting wise decision "seeds." Whether the results are good or bad is a direct result of the seed planted. Even the smallest decision can produce long-lasting and wide-ranging results.

When facing temptations having a negative downside, be cautious in planting a decision seed. The resulting harvest may have lingering and troublesome effects. The prophet Hosea gave a perfect example of the sorrow and regret produced by dabbling in things best left alone:

> They have planted the wind and will harvest the whirlwind. The stalks of grain wither and produce nothing to eat (Hosea 8:7, NLT).

We reap later than we sow

Farmers understand the laws of nature and plan their harvest based on known planting and harvesting timetables. Unfortunately, there is no regular timetable for the harvests of life.

Some decision "seeds" germinate almost immediately, spring-up, and produce fruit (sweet or bitter) quickly while others take weeks, months, years, or even decades to flourish. Your goal must be to produce fruit that benefits others, glorifies God, and creates a life worth following.

A Serious Warning

The *Law of the Harvest* provides clear benefits, but Scripture also includes this dire warning: "Do not be deceived, God is not mocked."

How can anyone mock God? Basically, a person mocks God by rationalizing personal exemption from any one (or more) of His laws.

- We mock God by ignoring and taking for granted the wonder of His creation.

- We mock God by disrespecting His Word and neglecting its counsel in day-to-day decisions.

- We mock God by pridefully believing we are more intelligent and forward-thinking than wisdom and common sense suggests.

- We mock God by believing we can "get by" in life without having a personal relationship with Jesus.

We can mock God by doing something we know is wrong and excusing ourselves by rationalizing, "It's not a big sin and besides, everybody else is doing it, so it really doesn't count."

The renowned psychologist William James[4] said: "You may not count it, but it is being counted, just the same. Down among your nerve cells and fibers the molecules are counting it, registering, storing it up to be used against you when the next temptation comes."

God is very aware of human weakness in the face of temptation. He understands that your desire for more and better may cause you to bend a few rules but cautions against self-deception.

Many people are deceived into not believing the truth or into thinking they are somehow the exception to God's laws. Do not allow yourself to fall into the trap of living carelessly just because you think everything will turn out okay.

God never gives anyone a *Get Out of Jail Free* card and in fact, speaks clearly and directly to the practice of rationalization and self-deception:

> When a crime is not punished quickly, people feel it is safe to do wrong. But even though a person sins a hundred times and still lives a long time, I know that those who fear God will be better off. The wicked will not prosper, for they do not fear God. Their days will never grow long like the evening shadows (Ecclesiastes 8:11-13, NLT).

Unleash the Power

The *Butterfly Effect* is constantly at work in your life. Not every flap of a butterfly's wings sets an air molecule in motion that initiates a process resulting in a destructive weather pattern...most flaps go gently unnoticed.

And so, it is with life. Our daily routine is so often mundane that its effects go unnoticed or ignored. We give little thought to how our actions—especially the small or insignificant ones—may have far-reaching effects. Truthfully, the little things you say and do are not unlike the constant flapping of a butterfly's wings...they often stir up meaningful results in other people's lives.

Read the following historical narrative, paying close attention to the details. and answer this question: Who made the most significant contribution to Jesus' opportunity to perform the miracle?

> After this, Jesus crossed over to the far side of the Sea of Galilee, also known as the Sea of Tiberias. A huge crowd kept following him wherever he went, because they saw his miraculous signs as he healed the sick. Then Jesus climbed a hill and sat down with his disciples around him. (It was nearly time for the Jewish Passover celebration.)
>
> Jesus soon saw a huge crowd of people coming to look for him. Turning

102

to Philip, he asked, "Where can we buy bread to feed all these people?" He was testing Philip, for he already knew what he was going to do. Philip replied, "Even if we worked for months, we wouldn't have enough money to feed them!"

Then Andrew, Simon Peter's brother, spoke up. "There's a young boy here with five barley loaves and two fish. But what good is that with this huge crowd?"

"Tell everyone to sit down," Jesus said. So they all sat down on the grassy slopes. (The men alone numbered about 5,000.) Then Jesus took the loaves, gave thanks to God, and distributed them to the people. Afterward he did the same with the fish.

And they all ate as much as they wanted. After everyone was full, Jesus told his disciples, "Now gather the leftovers, so that nothing is wasted. So they picked up the pieces and filled twelve baskets with scraps left by the people who had eaten from the five barley loaves (John 6:1-13, NLT).

You likely noted that several miracles occurred that afternoon but who made the major contribution permitting Jesus to turn a chaotic situation into a successful picnic? Probably not Philip. Was it Andrew, the guy who acquired the bread and fish? Or was it the little boy who shared his lunch?

Actually, the person responsible for making the picnic possible was likely not present at the event. *It was the boy's mother!* She arose early that morning and went about the unexciting chores of her daily routine.

After preparing breakfast and washing the dishes, this Mom must have given permission for her son to attend the meeting, made sure he was properly dressed, and as she prepared his lunch, undoubtedly prayed for his safe return home.

The *Power of Subservient Action* unleashed by this Mom's attention to the monotonous details of daily life centuries ago is embedded within your being!

Just as the *Power of Subservient Action* is subconsciously unleashed from routine activities, the *Power of Intentional Action* produces fruit via the *Law of the Harvest*. The good seeds of character planted into someone's life directly or by influence, take root, and activate the *Law of the Harvest*.

Plant Seeds of Character

History was forever altered on April 2, 1877 when Mordecai F. Ham[5] was born on a farm in Allen County, KY. Christ-centered seeds were planted early in his life, took root, flourished and created a never-ending ripple effect.

As an adult, Mordecai shared, "From the time I was eight years old, I never thought of myself as anything but a Christian. At nine, I had definite convictions that the Lord wanted me to preach...".

Mordecai entered the ministry in 1901 and became a well-known preacher in the Southeast United States. It has been estimated that more than 300,000 people were converted in his crusade-style meetings.

Local pastors and the Christian Men's Club in Charlotte, NC invited Dr. Ham to hold a series of revival meetings. The evangelist preached six days a week, morning and night, for eleven weeks. Thousands flocked to the ramshackle building with sawdust ground cover built especially for the occasion.

An unparalleled example of God's *Law of the Harvest* occurred during a meeting there on November 1, 1934. An almost-sixteen-year old boy named Billy Graham[6] responded to Ham's message, walked the aisle, and accepted Jesus Christ as his personal Savior!

Billy Graham became an evangelist and went on to preach to more people in person than anyone else in history—nearly 215 million people throughout the world. Dr. Graham's messages have touched millions more through television, video, film, and the Internet.

The legacies of Mordecai Ham and Billy Graham continue to ripple exponentially throughout history via the lives of people who accepted Jesus Christ as Savior through their ministry.

The harvest continues to proliferate as Franklin Graham[7]—Billy's son— continues to sow seeds into their legacies. He serves as an evangelist and President of Samaritan's Purse.

The Samaritan's Purse Operation Christmas Child (OCC) program received 10,569,405 shoeboxes in 2019 for distribution to children in 118 countries. The OCC program reported that 2.2 million decisions for Jesus Christ were recorded in 2019.

Tobias and Ollie Ham could not imagine the harvest God would produce from seeds they sowed in the life of their small son. Likewise, Mordecai Ham and Billy Graham could not foresee the far-reaching, never-ending effects of their preaching.

The legacy of these well-known preachers was developed over time by their day-by-day trust in God and obedience in doing what they knew He wanted them to do. That is all God asks of us...to trust and obey!

A Smooth Stone
All you can do is all you can do but with God, that's enough!

What's Next?

What you choose to do in the tomorrows of your life is important. *How* you do what you do is critical to your success. The "how" is a key element in strengthening the foundation of your legacy.

One important *how* is learning from other people and staying in touch with God. Memorize and apply the wisdom of this Scripture to every waking moment of your life:

> Work willingly at whatever you do, as though you were working for the Lord rather than for people (Colossians 3:23, NLT).

A Smooth Stone
The way you do anything is the way you do everything.

The future is coming! Are you ready to make it better than the future which has already become your past? Jim Rohn[8]—a wise student of life—encouraged us to excellence with this astute admonition:

> Let others lead small lives, but not you. Let others argue over small things, but not you. Let others cry over small hurts, but not you. Let others leave their future in someone else's hands, but not you.

Chapter Notes

1. Scripture records Shamgar was the third judge of Israel and "Shamgar... killed six hundred men of the Philistines with an ox-goad, and he also delivered Israel (Judges 3:31). An ox-goad was a wooden tool fitted with an iron spike or point at one end and was used to spur oxen as they pulled a plow or a cart.

2. Edward Norton Lorenz (1917–2008) was an American mathematician and meteorologist. Dr. Lorenz is widely acknowledged as the father of *The Chaos Theory* and *The Butterfly Effect*. Source: Lorenz, Edward N. (March 1963) *Deterministic Nonperiodic Flow*, Journal of the Atmospheric Sciences.

3. Source: North Carolina State University, County Extension Director-Horticulture, Mecklenburg County, NC. This analysis was received via an email on May 26, 2006.

4. William James (1842–1910) was an American philosopher and psychologist and the first educator to offer a psychology course in the United States.

5. Mordecai Ham (1877–1961) was a fiery American Independent Baptist evangelist and temperance movement leader. He entered the ministry in

1901 and in 1936 began a radio broadcast reaching into seven southern states. Sources: *Past Masters: Mordecai Ham: The Southern Revivalist* by David R. Stokes at www.preaching.com and www.wikipedia.com.

6. Billy Graham (1918–2018) was an American evangelist, a prominent evangelical Christian figure, and an ordained Southern Baptist minister who became internationally well-known beginning in the late 1940s.

7. Franklin Graham (b. 1952) is a Christian evangelist, missionary and serves as president and CEO of the Billy Graham Evangelistic Association and the international Christian organization, Samaritan's Purse.

8. Jim Rohn (1930–2009) was an American entrepreneur, author and motivational speaker. He entertainingly presented his philosophy of life via books and seminars.

Chapter 10
The Future is Coming

The best way to predict the future is to create it.
—Peter Drucker[1]

The only certainty of the future is its uncertainty!

Trying to predict the future is like trying to drive down a country road at night with no lights while looking out the back window.[1]

In early October, the renowned economist Irving Fisher[2] predicted, "Stock prices have reached what looks like a permanently high plateau." Since the Dow Jones Industrial Average (DJIA) had swelled to a record high several weeks earlier, he had good reason to believe his forecast was accurate.

Dr. Fisher's ecstasy over the DJIA's closing at 381.17 on September 3 was short-lived as the bubble began to burst on October 24, 1929. The market began a series of precipitous drops known as "black days" which led to The Great Depression—the worst economic downturn in the history of the industrialized world.

Our inability to see clearly what lies ahead can be frustrating and cause apprehension but unlike many people, Christians can face an uncertain future with calm certainty.

The Law of the Future

Everyone is born acutely unaware of a future beyond that which is physically observable. Unfortunately, many grow in chronological age and physical maturity without recognizing a natural law as certain as the Law of Gravity:

The future is coming, whether or not you are ready!

Our view of the future may be blurred by an undue focus on the past but our confidence in it is not dependent on personal experience or wisdom.

> Never be afraid to trust an unknown future to a known God.
> —Corrie ten Boom[3]

The future is not a mystery to God! He has a plan for your life, knows your every need and will listen attentively as you tell Him your troubles and seek His guidance.

> Eye has not seen, nor ear heard, nor have entered into the heart of man the things which God has prepared for those who love Him (1 Corinthians 2:9).

> Call to Me, and I will answer you, and show you great and mighty things, which you do not know (Jeremiah 33:3).

God knows every detail of your future. He wants you to partner with Him in aligning your life to match His plan for your legacy. As His partner, you are responsible for daily decisions that pave the way to a future in sync with His plan.

Visualize Your Future

The ancient philosopher Heraclitus said, "You can never step in the same river twice." Life is perpetually changing around us, but God remains constant and dependable. He can always be trusted to keep His promises and we can count on His unchanging faithfulness.

Have you visualized your future? Or have you assumed only prophets and super-saints can have a vision of the future? God's Word graphically defines the results of sailing into the future without a plan:

> Where there is no vision, the people perish; but he that keepeth the law, happy is he (Proverbs 29:18, KJV).

Self-help gurus recommend setting tangible goals and aspirations...and you should! However, as a Christian, your vision must go beyond seeking tangible results; you must focus on the life-changing effects your life can have on the lives of others.

Tangible goals and aspirations lead to outcomes determined by what you "do." The success of your vision will be determined by what you "be."

A Smooth Stone
*What you **be** is more important than what you **do**!*

Your view of the future will shape your present reality. The template for the present is created based on the value placed on past experience—*the known*—when making decisions about the *not-yet-known* future.

Be wary of making decisions based on outdated knowledge or habits cultivated over the years. You may be pre-conditioned to believe that yesterday's norm is an absolute precursor to tomorrow's certainty. The way something has always been done may not be the best way.

A character in Herman Wouk's[4] bestselling novel, *Marjorie Morningstar* observed, "Experience—nine times out of ten—is merely stupidity hardened into habit." Don't take this perspective personally; everyone has some experience grounded in a not-so-wise habit!

The disappointments and limitations of your past do exist but do not have to define or restrict the infinite possibilities of your future.

A Smooth Stone
The past is all fact. The future is all possibility!

Left unchecked, the future will automatically mold your past thought patterns into its reality. In essence, your past creates the present which becomes a tentative precursor of the future. Developing a life worth emulating may require assessing and creatively retooling the links in a chain of past experiences.

The most effective way to rework this natural chain of probability is to partner with God to serve as His conduit into the lives of others.

It is not what we gain but what He pours through us that really counts. God's purpose is not simply to make us beautiful, plump grapes, but to make us grapes so that He may squeeze the sweetness out of us. Our spiritual life cannot be measured by success as the world measures it, but only by what God pours through us—and we cannot measure that at all.[5]

The future cannot be clearly seen because we cannot yet clearly see God's total plan. Ask your Inner Coach to help you hone or develop these attributes to become an effective conduit for effecting His plan:

1. *Accept life as a process.* There will be ups 'n downs and life will not always agree with your opinion. Get over it! Learn to *relearn*, as necessary.

2. *Live a value-driven life.* Know what you believe and why. Keep your "I Believe" list up-to-date and use it as a guide for non-negotiable personal values and beliefs.

3. *Build your own personal brand.* Live a life of such substance and integrity that people will trust and respect you. Your personal brand—how others see you—is invaluable in living a life worth emulating.

4. *Become an observant servant.* Be sensitive to the needs of others even those you do not know personally. Anonymously meet as many needs as possible. Humility is a tremendous personal quality.

5. *Be an encourager.* Look for the good in others and compliment them often. Refuse to repeat innuendo or gossip.

6. *Be an empathetic listener.* Strive to accept and understand the uniqueness of others even when their opinion or behavior is disagreeable. Avoid the temptation to quash ideas you don't understand or find disagreeable. Be open to the idea that you may be mistaken.

7. *Live with purpose and passion.* As a Christian, your life should reflect

the attributes of Christ. The characteristics of goodness, kindness, mercy, compassion, gratitude, and thoughtfulness can be developed and should be readily apparent to anyone observing your lifestyle.

Work on developing daily habits consistent with your vision of becoming a person of greater value to the cause of Christ. Difficult people and obstinate obstacles will clutter the path, but your focus must remain on achieving your vision.

Three burly henchmen constantly work with Satan to quench your Christ-centered vision: These nemeses are procrastination, people, and fear.

Vision Quencher – Procrastination

People have struggled with procrastination since ancient times but many 21st Century Christians have mastered the process!

The effects of procrastination can run the gamut of humorous to devastating. Erma Bombeck[6] described the net effect of procrastination on personal dreams when she observed:

> There are people who put their dreams in a little box and say, "Yes, I have got dreams. Of course, I've got dreams!" Then they put the box away and bring it out once in a while to look in it, and yep, they're still there! These are great dreams, but they never even get out of the box.

Self-discipline and determination are often pushed to the sidelines when uncertainty, temptation, or a selfish attitude shows up. A predictable culprit will emerge: The simple habit of procrastination.

The unyielding urge to put-off something that is—or seems to be—important is a mysterious phenomenon. An invisible force keeps you from completing urgent and important tasks. The temptation to delay or postpone action is strong, like trying to push the opposing poles of a super-strong magnet together.

The urge to procrastinate may come from overestimating the size and difficulty of a task or opportunity. The old adage, "you can't see the forest for the trees," suggests too much focus is on the details. It would be like needing to paint your house in one day but spending the first half of the day picking-out the right color. Take a macro view, decide...and act!

When the results of a decision are unpredictable, ask yourself these three questions:
1. What is the best thing that could happen?
2. What is the worst thing that could happen?
3. What is the most likely thing to happen?

If the most likely thing to happen is the worst thing that could happen, but you could live with it, you may choose to go for it!

If you cannot live with the worst thing that could happen, choose to not do it! This is a wise decision, not procrastination.

When the allure of procrastination arrives, visualize your future self. Would the temporary pleasure of putting something off be more gratifying than the satisfaction of completing a worthwhile task?

Leaving your dreams (vision) in the box will almost always lead to the psychological pain of disappointment and regret. At a minimum, procrastination is annoying and disappointing. At its extreme, it can be the source of incessant, painful regret.

The American philosopher Jim Rohn made this astute observation:

> We must all suffer from one of two pains: the pain of discipline or the pain of regret. The difference is discipline weighs *ounces* while regret weighs *tons*.

Postpone procrastination! Be bold in making your vision a reality! Step outside your comfort zone. If overwhelming chaos does not occur, take another step...and another!

114

Vision Quencher – People

There is a scene in *Man of La Mancha* where Don Quixote and Sancho Panza are gazing wistfully at a dilapidated inn. When Quixote describes his vision by comparing the building to the Alcazar, the magnificent royal palace in Seville, his servant tries hard to see his master's vision but can only see ruins.

As his servant attempts to describe what he sees, Quixote tells him to stop, saying, "I will not allow your facts to interfere with my vision!"

There is probably at least one Sancho Panza in your life.

When the dream of your vision begins to come out of its box, you may expect surprising responses from family and friends. There will be no shortage of naysayers to dampen or disparage your enthusiasm.

Your Sancho Panza will offer *opinions* thinly disguised as *facts* to dissuade or discourage you. Watch for these predictable characteristics in your friends, family, and acquaintances:

A Smooth Stone
Everybody is either wind in your sail, or an anchor on your tail.

Stay encouraged! You and God are a winning partnership working to make the vision of your renewed life a reality. When you feel overwhelmed, remember:

> The things which are impossible with men are possible with God (Luke 18:27).

Vision Quencher – Fear

Fear is a natural enemy; a formidable adversary determined to crush your dreams and annihilate your vision. It is often simply an emotion for you to overcome.

Fear is usually nothing more than an *illusion* manifesting itself as *worry*. The great French philosopher, Montaigne, observed: "My life," he said, "has been full of terrible misfortunes most of which never happened."

Everyone is born with two innate fears: the fear of falling and the fear of loud noises. Every other fear must be *learned* and can therefore be *unlearned*.

Certain fears will recur because you have developed a habit of compensating for them. If you begin facing a fear rather than compensating for it, you will develop habits that negate it.

There is a term in bullfighting called a *querencia*. It is a spot that a bull always returns to in the ring when he feels vulnerable. Every bull has a specific querencia—each is different, but every bull has one.

Likewise, every person has a querencia, a *comfort zone*, a safe haven retreat insulating us from certain fears. The only way to venture outside your querencia is to have a vision so compelling that leaving your comfort zone is worth the accompanying risk.

The French-born American author, Anaïs Nin[7] gave this poetic example:

> And the day came when the risk to remain tight in a bud was more painful than the risk it took to blossom.

The most repeated command in the Bible is said to be, "Fear not!" Lloyd Ogilive[8] says there are 366 "fear nots" in the Bible – one for every day of the year, including Leap Year! He suggests God does not want us to go even one day without hearing His word of comfort, "Fear not!"

God thoughtfully and beautifully provides nuggets of courage to alleviate any threat or fear we may encounter. These kernels of truth are found in Scripture:

> For I am the LORD your God who takes hold of your right hand and says to you, do not fear, I will help you (Isaiah 41:13, NIV).

> Have I not commanded you? Be strong and of good courage; do not be afraid, nor be dismayed, for the LORD your God is with you wherever you go (Joshua 1:9).

I sought the LORD, and He heard me, and delivered me from all my fears (Psalm 34:4).

For God has not given us a spirit of fear, but of power and of love and of a sound mind (2 Timothy 1:7).

Cast your burden on the LORD, and He shall sustain you; He shall never permit the righteous to be moved (Psalm 55:22).

The LORD is my light and my salvation—whom shall I fear? The LORD is the stronghold of my life—of whom shall I be afraid? (Psalm 27:1, NIV).

There is no fear in love; but perfect love casts out fear because fear involves torment. But he who fears has not been made perfect in love (1 John 4:18).

The LORD is on my side; I will not fear. What can man do to me? (Psalm 118:6).

Finally, trust in and rely on the promises of God. He has promised to never leave you nor forsake you (*see* Hebrews 13:5) and to meet your every need (*see* Philippians 4:19). Since God *cannot* lie, He will keep every one of His promises! (*See* Titus 1:2).

Trust God and neglect naysayers! Spend time with encouragers. There are many—including some you can never know personally—who would like to help you succeed. Tap into their invaluable cache of personal experiences.

Chapter Notes

1. Peter Drucker (1909–2005) was an American-Austrian management consultant, author, and educator.

2. Dr. Irving Fisher, Professor of Economics, Yale University. Source: Time Magazine, September 3, 2014; additional source, history.com.

3. Corrie ten Boom (1892–1983) was a Dutch Christian watchmaker and writer. During WWII, she and her family helped many Jews escape the Nazis and avoid the Holocaust by hiding them in their home.

4. Herman Wouk (1915–2019) was a Pulitzer Prize-winning American author best known for historical fiction.

5. Oswald Chambers (1874–1917) was a Scottish born teacher and preacher. This quote is from *My Utmost for His Highest,* September 2.

6. Erma Bombeck (1927–1996) Erma Louise Bombeck was an American humorist who achieved popularity for her newspaper column from the mid-1960s until the late 1990s. She also published 15 books.

7. Anaïs Nin (1903–1977) was a French-Cuban American diarist, essayist, novelist, and writer of short stories.

8. Lloyd John Ogilvie (1930–2019) was a Presbyterian minister and served as the 61st Chaplain of the United States Senate from 1995 through 2004. The quote is from Ogilvie's book, *Facing the Future Without Fear.*

Chapter 11
Secondhand Hindsight

*The first thing is to find out everything that everybody else knows,
and then begin where they left off.*
—Thomas Edison

Infinite wisdom and knowledge reside in the collective 20/20 hindsight reservoirs of other people. If asked, many will eagerly share thoughts, ideas, and wisdom to help you have a more meaningful life.

A Smooth Stone
*You are smart when you learn from experience.
You are wise when you learn from other people's experiences.*

Have you ever wondered what successful persons from disparate backgrounds would share if asked to share perspectives on how to prepare for the future?

Escape from Success

He achieved success by earning a scholarship and attending Brown University—graduating with honors—followed by a Juris Doctor degree, again with honors. Proud to have served as a Company Commander in the Marines and later becoming a senior partner in a large and thriving law firm, he was on top of the world!

At age 39, this grandson of an immigrant was named an assistant to the President, with an office immediately next to his. His life was the American Dream fulfilled!

> It was only when I achieved all of those things that I realized how empty they really were. I was seeking to find meaning in life through power, influence, money, stature and politics, and I failed. I had success but I also had a tremendous hole inside of me. I discovered that it was a spiritual vacuum.

In prison with all the things of this world stripped away, I found the only security and meaning and purpose a person ever knows—a personal relationship with the living God, Jesus Christ.

On looking back, I can honestly say that I never met anyone the entire time I was in government who told me that their life had been affected by anything I had done—at least for the good. By contrast, I've met hundreds, maybe thousands, since I've been in Christian service, whose lives God has chosen to touch through my life and largely through my biggest defeat, going to prison.

How would I today define success? Certainly not the way I did in the first forty years of my life. Now, success to me is believing, following and serving God, and being at peace with Him. I keep a plaque on my desk that reminds me of what I believe to be the principal calling of the Christian. It reads "Faithfulness Not Success."

Chuck Colson[1] voluntarily pled guilty to obstruction of justice on a Watergate-related charge and served seven months in prison. In his best-selling memoir, *Born Again*, he wrote, "I found myself increasingly drawn to the idea that God had put me in prison for a purpose and that I should do something for those I had left behind."

Emerging from prison, Chuck had a new mission: mobilizing Christians to minister to prisoners, former prisoners, and their families. He founded *Prison Fellowship Ministries* in 1976.

Unexpected Expectations

Not yet 23-years-old on August 26, 1968, Nicky Daniel "Nick" Bacon[2] found himself in a dangerous and scary situation just west of Tam Ky, Vietnam. When his group came under fire from an enemy bunker, Nick advanced on the hostile bunker and destroyed it with grenades. As he did so, several comrades including his platoon leader were struck by machine-gun fire and fell wounded.

Staff Sergeant Bacon immediately assumed command of the platoon and assaulted the hostile gun position finally killing the enemy gun crew in a single-handed effort.

When the 3rd Platoon moved to Staff Sergeant Bacon's location, its leader was immediately wounded. Without hesitation, Staff Sergeant Bacon took charge of the additional platoon and continued the fight.

In the ensuing action, he personally killed four more enemy soldiers and silenced an antitank weapon. While several wounded soldiers were being evacuated, Nick continued to ignore the intense hostile fire and climbed up on the exposed deck of a tank to direct firepower into the enemy position.

Nick Bacon was awarded our Nation's highest military decoration, the Medal of Honor, for his heroic actions in that day's combat experience.

After retiring from a 20-year Army career, Nick became a businessman and served as president of the *Congressional Medal of Honor Society*. His passion for helping others succeed is reflected in this personal testimony:

> In combat, my faith in God grew, as did my respect for the word 'honor.' I wish I could sit down at a campfire with all of our nation's young people and they would listen to my words of advice. They are simple words; No one is perfect, everyone fails and often comes a little short of what we expect of ourselves.
>
> I have traveled the world and have seen many places and different races of people. I trained years for war and fought in the dark jungles of Vietnam. Yet, I know so little, I feel so small. I have searched for strength and found weakness. I have found the true and everlasting strength only through faith in my God.

I have found that, through prayer, I am a giant of power and ability. But faith is not something that just happens, you must develop it. With faith you can move a mountain, keep a family together, help a friend, or even win a war.

If you desire spiritual greatness, you must humble yourself, set aside all your human pride, study the Word of God, and always be in prayer.

By any metric, Nick Bacon is a true patriot and an authentic American hero, whose legacy continues to influence people he never knew.

Know and Go

Many boys dream of becoming a major league baseball player; a lesser number hope to become a medical doctor. It is *exceptionally* rare for a youth to have both aspirations.

Bobby Brown[3] was that exception, and he was successful! Over the nine seasons between 1946 and 1954, Bobby played eight for the New York Yankees. During his baseball career, the Yankees participated in—and won—six World Series Championships and Bobby Brown graduated from medical school!

Bobby believes the foundation for living a life worth following and creating a lasting legacy requires dreaming big, believing in yourself, and never giving up. His advice is, "*Know* what you want and *go* for it!"

What I have tried to tell young people is not to be afraid to dream big. If they have a desire to accomplish something, don't let anyone discourage them from trying. No dream, no matter how far-fetched, is impossible.

The world is full of negative people who tend to discourage young people if their dreams and ambitions seem out of reach. Young people should not be swayed by the negative opinions of their friends and advisors.

If a young person has a particular aim in life, he or she should be prepared to work exceedingly hard and go for it. There may come a time when the dream has to be abandoned, but that decision should be made by the person involved. Young people should always remember—anything is possible. In this country there is no limit to one's dreams.

Except for my parents and myself, there was no one who thought I could go to medical school and play major league baseball at the same time. Fortunately, I was able to convince the dean of my medical school (Tulane) to let me try.

I had already demonstrated that I could handle the workload in medical school. And in my heart, I thought I could hit any pitcher on the face of the earth. It was hard work, but it all worked out. I played with the Yankees while I was in medical school and while I interned.

In addition to his baseball and medical careers, Bobby Brown served as president of Major League Baseball's American League (1984 –1994).

A Heart for Hearts

Dr. Denton A. Cooley[4] was a world-renowned cardiovascular surgeon and founder of the Texas Heart Institute. He began his career after graduating from Johns Hopkins University School of Medicine. He performed the first successful heart transplant in the United States in 1968 and in 1969, became the first surgeon to implant an artificial heart in a human being.

Throughout his life, this distinguished physician maintained a vital interest in encouraging young people to prepare for the future.

I am a firm believer in educating and preparing young adults for life beyond the illusions of safety and security in an ideal world. As many before me have stated, the only real cure for combating ignorance is acquiring knowledge.

To acquire knowledge at this critical stage of life, young adults must have self-discipline: the self-discipline to continue their education, to develop a strong work ethic, to learn when to take risks, and to stand up for their rights.

But it is not enough to mature intellectually. With the growing number of health concerns, such as the threat of AIDS, cardiovascular disease, and obesity, it is especially vital that *everyone*, young and old alike, learn to practice healthy habits. From personal hygiene to personal health, research and innovations of the 21st century have allowed mankind to improve his welfare. Young adults should take advantage of this new knowledge to live healthful lives.

In this period of discord, it is important for young Americans to commit to a sense of unity. Yet, to keep the identity of humanity strong, youths must continue to develop and foster their senses of duty to themselves, to their parents, to their friends, to their fellow neighbors, and, yes, even to their enemies. It then befalls on this generation of youth to continue to eradicate that ill disease known as ignorance. Today's *educated* young adults must teach the next generation of youngsters how to prepare for life. This is how we can allow everyone to achieve his or her dreams.

The wise counsel Dr. Cooley wrote to young adults is also applicable to Christians of every age seeking to live a life worth following and leaving a lasting legacy.

An Opportune Decision

She had modest ambitions when she decided to jump-start her life by joining the Navy. As it turned out, her timing was impeccable; the Navy was entering a period of significant changes in tradition.

Darlene Iskra[5] was one of the first female line officers to graduate from the Naval School of Diving and Salvage and in December 1990, became the first woman to assume command of a United States Navy ship, the USS *Opportune* (ARS 41). By the time she retired in April 2000, after 21 years of service, she had attained the rank of Commander.

When asked, "What advice would you give to encourage people in planning the pursuit of their dreams?" she responded:

> I have to say that I have not stopped learning...every time I do something new, I make mistakes all over again! So, I guess my advice would be thus:
>
> 1. Never stop learning.
>
> 2. Never stop trying new things...challenge yourself.
>
> 3. Keep an open mind. Just because things have "always been done that way" doesn't make it the most effective or the most efficient way.
>
> 4. Keep your perspective and don't take things personally.
>
> I wish I could say I have all sorts of wisdom to impart, but I really don't. If I had it to do again, I would be less selfish, more understanding, less rigid, more loving, concerned about doing a good job at my job but more concerned about making a good family life.
>
> I wouldn't take myself so seriously, and I would take my

personal commitments and family more seriously. I would question my priorities and re-evaluate them often.

Last of all, even though mistakes are made, I learn from them and try to do better in the future.

Commander Iskra's wise counsel for making life-altering decisions are timeless and applicable to everyone.

Generally Speaking

Nicknamed "Stormin' Norman," General H. Norman Schwarzkopf[6] was known for his fiery temper and his keen strategic mind. He was a 1956 graduate of West Point where he participated in the chapel choir and on the football and wrestling teams.

Schwarzkopf volunteered to fight in the Vietnam War and earned three Silver Stars, a Bronze Star and a Purple Heart. He retired from the United States Army as a four-star general.

General Schwarzkopf's insight can be helpful as you seek to live a life worth following:

> Concerning what my message might be to student athletes to encourage them in planning their pursuit of the American Dream in today's world, I guess the best answer I can give is in three parts.

- We are lucky to live in America. In most other nations, by the time you have reached high school, it is already predetermined what your future profession might be. In America, you are blessed because you can be whatever you choose to be if you are willing to pay the price in the doing.

- Plain and simple, no matter how tough it gets, never quit.

- Always remember that you can't help someone up a hill without getting a little closer to the top yourself.

General Schwarzkopf's life experiences uniquely qualified him to offer advice on preparing for the future and being a blessing to others.

Character Counts

During his 36 years in the Marine Corps, Charles Krulak[7] served tours of duty in the Vietnam War, the Gulf War, Operation Desert Shield, and Operation Desert Storm. These wartime experiences made an indelible impression on his philosophy of life.

> If I had a message for the youth of today, it would be a simple one—to be successful in life, you must be a man or woman of Character. Here I define Character as being selfless, having great moral courage and having a strong sense of integrity.
>
> Traits such as virtue, intelligence, physical courage, persistence, flexibility, articulation, etc. are all gifts—if you are a Christian, these are all gifts from God. If you are not a Christian, these come from heredity.
>
> Character is *not* a gift. Character is a choice. Character is built by making the "right" decision time after time. You build a reservoir of Character so that in the toughest of times, you are able to reach deep within yourself and draw upon this reservoir of Character and succeed.
>
> Your victories will be sweet! Your victories will stand the test of time! Your victories will inspire others! When you are a leader, you are in the inspiration business. You inspire ordinary people to do extraordinary things.

General Krulak emphasized that personal integrity and character are personal choices and necessary components of a life worth following!

A Message from Grunt

Charles "Grunt" Smith[8] served many years as a Naval aviator, logging more than 4,600 flight hours and 596 carrier arrestments while piloting 32 different fixed and rotary-wing aircraft. In April 2003, Captain Smith assumed command of the nuclear-powered aircraft carrier, USS *Dwight D. Eisenhower* (CVN 69). While on this assignment, he shared these personal perspectives on what is required to have a satisfying, successful life:

> I have three sons, two high school and college rowers and one who climbs tall peaks and runs the Boston marathon for "fun." One is a Navy jet pilot like me, one an Army helo pilot, and my youngest is still in high school.
>
> As you know, I also care for another 2800 young men and women. To them all, I tell them to measure themselves honestly and critically by the standards of the Ten Commandments and our Nation's Constitution.
>
> For success, true personal and professional happiness and the respect that comes from a humble life, they need not look for any other metric. The standards haven't changed; it just takes more guts and integrity to meet them today.

With one minor revision, Captain Smith's *Command Direction* to the "Ike" Sailors fits nicely into your plans for creating a lasting legacy:

> In the pursuit of Total Combat Readiness (read as, a life worth emulating), we will be unrelenting. When called into harm's way, we stand together and *never say die!*

A Creative Perspective

He has been credited with saving thousands from choking to death. Challenging accepted protocol for clearing a choking person's airways, i.e. slapping them on the back, he believed the process could actually worsen the problem.

Seeking a safer way to clear an obstruction, Dr. Henry Heimlich[9] invented a simple procedure. His ingenious process, widely known as the *Heimlich Maneuver* is credited with saving many lives each year.

This pioneer in innovative medical treatments offered his advice for living a goals focused life:

> All humans have the potential to be creative. If all of your peers understand what you've done, you haven't been creative. Most people go along with the crowd whether right or wrong.
>
> You can only be creative if you have the courage and honesty to overcome attacks by your colleagues and the public.
>
> A recent example is the use of the Heimlich Maneuver to save drowning victims. The Maneuver has been proven to clear water from the lungs, thus enabling drowning victims to breathe and survive.
>
> Powerful first aid organizations, for more than fifty years, have impressed into the minds of the public the use of CPR to resuscitate drowning victims. Rather than admit to the fatal error of trying to blow air into the victim's water-filled lungs, they have attacked the use of the Maneuver as the first step in saving the lives of drowning victims.
>
> My advice to the younger generation is to stand by your convictions and persevere until you attain your goal.

A key element of Dr. Heimlich's advice is to remain resolute in the face of criticism from the naysayers in your world.

The Essential Doorknob

Paul Galanti's[10] A-4C Skyhawk fighter bomber was shot down during his

97th combat mission. Although he could see the rescue destroyers offshore, the plane went out of control before he could reach them. Later that day—June 17, 1966—he was captured and began a 2,432-day ordeal as a Prisoner of War (POW) in Hanoi, North Vietnam.

Much later, he shared these thoughts for young people to consider when looking to the future:

> What I know now after my experience is that there are some really bad people in the world who cannot be changed, e.g. Communists and terrorists—they cannot be rehabilitated.

> Re pursuing dreams: *Go for it!* In this country, *anybody* can do *anything*. Unfortunately, many try to do everything and waste their lives pursuing shadows instead of focusing on the only truly important things in life: family, friends and a relationship with God. Everything else pales.

"There is no such thing as a bad day when there's a doorknob on the inside of the door." —Commander Paul Galanti, USN (Retired.)

An Unarmed Hero

He was called a coward but earned the Medal of Honor. Desmond Doss[11] was a committed Christian who refused to kill or even carry a weapon yet won the military's highest award for heroism. He preferred to be known as a noncombatant rather than being labeled by the draft board's designation of "conscientious objector."

As a Seventh Day Adventist, he was ridiculed and scorned by officers and enlisted men for refusing to work on Saturdays. Some threw shoes at him while he prayed at his bunk and one told him, "Doss, if we ever get into combat, I am going to kill you."

He became a medic whose heroics on an Okinawa battlefield are legendary. Cited for repeated acts of bravery from April 29 to May 21, 1945, Desmond

Doss was awarded the Medal of Honor by President Harry S. Truman.

The moral and physical courage demonstrated by this humble Christian is unparalleled. He wrote this letter on March 8, 2004.

> Dear Mr. Newell:
>
> Thank you for your letter of some time ago. I don't always keep up with answering mail as soon as I should.
>
> You spoke of inspirational examples, and that is really what I want to write about. I believe in thinking and doing what I feel the Lord would have me think and do. So, this is my message:
>
> It is not how much you know but what you do with what you know that makes you a success in life and living. Please give your best to God and country.
>
> Let your light shine for Jesus. If we miss heaven, we have missed everything. So, give your life to Jesus every day and He will lead you in the way it is best for you to go.
>
> "Eye hath not seen nor ear heard, neither have entered into the heart of man, the things which God hath prepared for them that love Him" (1 Corinthians 2:9).
>
> Sincerely, your friend,
>
> Desmond T. Doss, CMH (signed)

Desmond Doss' extraordinary life is well documented in the 2016 biographical war drama, *Hacksaw Ridge*, directed by Mel Gibson.

The Miracle Mile

On May 6, 1954, England's Roger Bannister became the first runner to break the four-minute mile. His record of 3:59.4 minutes lasted for just over one month. On June 21, Australia's John Landy[12] smashed the world record when he ran 3:57.9 at a race in Finland.

On August 7, the only two sub-four-minute-mile runners in history approached the starting blocks for a race promoted as *The Miracle Mile.*

With only 90 yards to go in perhaps the world's most memorable race, John Landy glanced over his left shoulder to check on Bannister's position. At that instant, Bannister streaked by him to victory at 3:58:8. Landy's second-place finish at 3:59.6 marked the first time the four-minute mile had been broken by two runners in the same race.

John Landy graciously shared his perspectives on life with me:

> Most of us have a feeling that we are inadequate, that other people can do things, scholastically, artistically or physically, that we just could not do. But I believe everybody has some gift, some talent, and we all have a responsibility to seek it out and to nurture it. We need to focus on what we have and from the success that flows from this, we gain confidence and our character and attitude to life changes.
>
> In my experience, three factors all beginning with 'p' are the key—passion, perseverance and presentation. You will never succeed at anything unless you passionately believe in what you are trying to do. This is demonstrated in sport and in the professional careers of successful people.
>
> But life will always be a series of frustrations and without perseverance, tenacity, call it what you will, you will never succeed in achieving your goals. There should be no such words as, "I can't."

It is also important that, under pressure, we are able to deliver, to present, because again, life doesn't always allow us a long time to plan and deliver our objectives. You have to prepare yourself to be able, like a champion athlete, to deliver your best performance, sometimes at very short notice on a given day.

However, I believe there is much more to life than individual success and if we haven't helped others along the way and made a contribution to our community as a whole, then we have failed.

Immediately after the race, *Time* magazine quoted Landy as saying, "If I hadn't looked back, I would have won the race." However, in a letter dated October 24, 2005, John Landy's Personal Assistant wrote:

The Governor appreciates your enquiry concerning the quote attributed to him in *Time* magazine and can assure you that he would never have made such a comment at that time or subsequently. He has always acknowledged that, despite his looking back at a crucial moment, Roger Bannister ran the better race on the day.

John Landy's humility and wise counsel communicate the critical importance of a person's character in developing a life worth emulating.

A Husker's Perspective

After a brief NFL career, Tom Osborne[13] was named Nebraska's head football coach. The 1973 season began a 25-year career of remarkable success that ended poetically with a win in his final game, the 1998 Orange Bowl. After serving three terms in Congress, Tom returned to the University of Nebraska as Athletic Director.

Based on many years' experience working with collegiate athletes, Tom shared this perspective on planning for the future:

Education is something many young people take for granted,

but I feel that an education is extremely important to the development of an individual. I have talked with a lot of football players who wish they had never dropped out of school. But I have never talked with someone who wished they had quit school.

Abstinence from alcohol and drugs is also an important characteristic of a leader. I made a decision about abstinence in the ninth grade when a friend asked me to share a six-pack of beer on a fall weekend. I declined, but my friend began a cycle of drinking that would take over his life. He lost his wife, his career and eventually his life, all because of one wrong decision in the ninth grade.

Leaders tell the truth. I appreciate the truth because it gives me a reason to trust people. By the same token, those who lie can rarely be trusted again.

Finally, a spiritual life is a necessary component for a multi-dimensional person. Many young men I coached left school early for careers in the National Football League, believing they had achieved the American dream of money, talent, celebrity and youth. But after their football careers, many were one-dimensional because they had an education but no spiritual grounding.

These characteristics of education, abstinence from alcohol and drugs, truthfulness, and spirituality are not easily attained. It is also important to remind people that there will be times when their commitment to these values will be tested.

Choosing to develop the attributes outlined by Tom Osborne will lead you to a successful life and a lasting legacy.

The Speaker Speaks

As a politician, historian, author, and former Speaker of the United States House of Representatives, Newt Gingrich[14] provides a unique perspective on the key elements of success.

> My thoughts for young people in planning the pursuit of their dreams for the future include:
>
> *Dream Big:* If you don't have the courage to dream big, why would you expect to have big results?
>
> *Work Hard:* If you don't work hard, why are you dreaming big?
>
> *Learn Every Day:* If you don't learn every day, you can't possibly deal with the world because it's changing every day.
>
> *Enjoy Life:* If you don't enjoy life, you're not going to be able to sustain your energy level. If you're not doing something you feel good about, you can't put the time and energy into it.
>
> *Be True to Yourself:* Nobody else can validate you but you.

Newt's advice is directed to young people, but his recommendations are applicable to anyone of any age.

A Journalist's Perspective

It was a balmy December evening as Frank and Kay strolled with a friend along the beach after a dinner party at the Officer's Club. Observing heat flashes of lightning, the friend made this prophetic remark, "Just like the calm before the storm."

Early the next morning, Frank was awakened by the growing intensity of explosions. As a war correspondent, he was quick to get outside and make an early assessment of the situation. As a result, this young journalist filed what is believed to have been the first eyewitness account of the bombing of Pearl Harbor on December 7, 1941.

While Frank filed the first news reports of the attack, his wife, Kay, was dictating the first eyewitness accounts of the bombing. Frank Tremaine[15] was the *United Press* (later to become *UPI*) bureau manager in Honolulu on that infamous Sunday morning. He filed daily reports during the entire war in the Pacific and was aboard the USS *Missouri* (BB 63) in 1945 to witness Japan's signing of their surrender agreement.

Nearly sixty-three years later, Frank Tremaine shared his ideas on the necessary components for planning a successful future.

> Without regard to Pearl Harbor or the rest of the war, if I were to advise a young person on planning his/her future, I would stress the importance of the following:
>
> - *Honesty*. The importance of earning and meriting the trust of others cannot be overemphasized.
>
> - *Dedication*. Dedication to the task at hand. Dedication to one's ideals. Never quit. Was it John Paul Jones who said, "Don't give up the ship."?
>
> - *Think and plan*. A man without a plan is a rudderless ship. One who thinks ahead, who anticipates the reactions of others has a big advantage over any who don't. As in physics, every action creates a reaction and he who is prepared for the reaction, or several reactions, usually is the winner whether it is checkers, chess, athletic, business or war or happiness at home. Be prepared for your moments of crisis or opportunity.
>
> - *Count on a Higher Power*. It's surprising how often Something intercedes just when you thought all was lost.

• *Communicate.* Be sure everyone involved is fully informed. Your partners, teammates, family should know the plan, their part in it, and the parts that others are expected to play. If they know the plan, they can think too. If something goes wrong, criticize in private. If it goes right, praise in public. If you're not the captain, then you need to know what the captain's plan is.

• *Don't worry.* It interferes with thinking, planning and preparation. If you've thought, planned and prepared, forget the worry and go to sleep. Let the Higher Power worry, and you might be surprised.

As a newsman, I tried always to be skeptical but never cynical. A cynic is biased and it's impossible to report accurately from a position of bias. But skeptical questioning and research from a neutral position is essential for accurate reporting or success in any field. In life, however, sometimes faith must replace skepticism for faith carries us beyond doubt. This applies whether you're a newsperson, doctor, lawyer, beggarman or thief.

• *Know your history.* Know what happened and why, not only in this country but throughout the world. What happened in the past affects what's happening now. Knowledge of geography helps, too. Most dates are not very important but what, how and why are. This nation made many mistakes (Blacks, Indians, Viet Nam) but it's still the best. Why?

We are blessed to have access to Frank Tremaine's legacy of wisdom accumulated over a long and adventurous life.

A Coach's Perspective

Thirty-five college basketball coaches have more career wins than John Wooden[16] but he ranks Number One in influencing his players—and scores of other people—to make lasting, life-changing decisions. In spite of his legendary status as a coach, John Wooden seemed proudest to be a teacher, mentor, and friend.

Coach Wooden always found the time to make positive contributions to another person's life. Some years ago, I asked his advice on how student-athletes could plan for a successful future. His response is dated May 17, 2006:

> Dear Mr. Newell,
>
> When I graduated from a small country grade school in 1924, my father gave me a three by five card and said, "Son, try to live up to the suggestions made on this card."
>
> Being imperfect, I have failed on occasion, but I have tried and am certain that in doing so, I am a better person than I would have been.
>
> The enclosed card* lists the things that were on the card my father gave to me.
>
> In my opinion, retirement simply means a change in profession—so stay busy and do what you can to help others and you will have peace within and will be ready when the Master calls.
>
> Sincerely,
>
> John Wooden (signed)

*The card's wisdom is worth remembering:
• Happiness begins where selfishness ends.

- If I am through learning, I am through.
- Treat all people with dignity and respect.
- Make each day your masterpiece.
- What is right is more important than who is right.

A Call to Action

Think about what you've just read. Sixteen individuals from varied backgrounds and generations selflessly invested part of *their* life to help *you* have a better life!

Take a few minutes to carefully read their wisdom and advice again. Consider which bits of wisdom "speak" to you and underline, circle, and/or highlight those you choose to include in your personal philosophy of life.

From Here to Your Future

The choices and decisions those individuals made on a daily basis culminated in a personal legacy that continues beyond themselves to inspire and bless countless others.

Likewise, your choices and decisions will culminate in a legacy that can positively affect the lives of your family, friends, and hopefully, many people you will never meet.

You may need self-analysis to reveal the lifestyle changes necessary for a life worth emulating. Ask your Inner Coach to show you the wise choices that will please Him and bless others.

Chapter Notes

1. Charles W. "Chuck" Colson (1931–2012) served as Special Counsel to President Richard Nixon from 1969 to 1970. In 1974, he voluntarily pled guilty to obstruction of justice on a Watergate-related charge and served seven months in an Alabama prison. Source: Personal correspondence dated July 31, 2003.

2. Nicky Daniel "Nick' Bacon (1945–2010) served in the United States Army 1964–1984. Source: Personal correspondence dated July 21, 2003.

3. Robert W. Brown (b. 1924) played professional baseball for the New York Yankees and was a practicing cardiologist. Source: Personal correspondence dated January 5, 2004.

4. Denton A. Cooley (1920–2016) was a world-renowned surgeon and a pioneer in cardiovascular surgery. Source: Personal correspondence dated July 2, 2003.

5. Commander Darlene M. Iskra retired from the United States Navy in 2000, after 21 years of service. Source: Personal correspondence dated December 12, 2006.

6. H. Norman Schwarzkopf (1934–2012) graduated from West Point in 1956 and retired from active military service as a four-star general in 1991. Source: Personal correspondence dated April 28, 2003.

7. Charles C. Krulak (b. 1942) graduated from the United States Naval Academy in 1964 and retired as a four-star United States Marine Corps general in 1999. He served as the 31st Commandant of the Marine Corps. Source: Personal correspondence dated December 5, 2003.

8. After a 34-year career, Charles E. "Grunt" Smith retired as a Rear Admiral from the United States Navy in January 2013. Source: Personal correspondence dated July 14, 2003.

9. Henry J. Heimlich (1920–2016) was an American thoracic surgeon and medical researcher. In the early 1960s, Dr. Heimlich invented a device for draining fluid from open chest wounds. *The Heimlich Chest Drain Valve* was used by medics during the Vietnam War. Source: Personal correspondence dated May 4, 2004.

10. Paul E. Galanti (b. 1939) was a Prisoner of War in North Vietnam

from June 1966 to February 1973. He retired from the United States Navy as a Commander and served as the second Commissioner of the Virginia Department of Veterans Services. Source: Personal correspondence dated August 7, 2006.

11. Desmond T. Doss (1919–2006) was an Army medic during WWII. On the battlefield in Okinawa, he heroically saved the lives of more than seventy-five of his comrades. Source: Personal correspondence dated March 8, 2004.

12. John Landy (b. 1930) was the second runner to run the mile in less than four minutes. He was also the 26th Governor of Victoria Australia from 2001 to 2006. Source: Personal correspondence dated November 28, 2003.

13. Thomas William Osborne (b. 1937) is a former football player, coach, college athletics administrator, and politician from Nebraska. Source: Personal correspondence dated July 30, 2003.

14. Newton "Newt" Gingrich (b. 1943) is an American politician, historian, and author who served as the 50th Speaker of the United States House of Representatives. Source: Personal correspondence dated November 18, 2003.

15. Frank Tremaine (1914–2006) was the *United Press* bureau manager based in Honolulu throughout WWII. Source: Personal correspondence dated August 26, 2003.

16. John Wooden (1910–2010) was a three-time All-American basketball player (Purdue) who became legendary as head coach of the UCLA Bruins (1948–1975). Source: Personal correspondence dated May 17, 2006.

Chapter 12
The Keys to Your Legacy

*The greatest use of life is to spend it
on something that will outlast it.*
—William James[1]

Have you ever felt you were born a *nobody* in a *somebody* world? Do you sometimes feel totally insignificant? God has given 100% assurance that you are anything but insignificant!

You are a one-of-a-kind individual, created in God's own image (*see* Genesis 1:27) with a unique genetic code and fingerprints. Ethel Waters[2] was right-on when she affirmed, "I am somebody cause God don't make no junk!"

> Don't be afraid to think too highly of yourself. If the Creator made you and is not ashamed of the job, certainly you should not be. He pronounced His work 'good,' and you should respect it.
>
> —Orison Swett Marden[3]

We learn early in childhood that others have an impact on us but many of us are middle-aged—or older—before understanding that we have an impact on others.

You may see yourself as insignificant, but you are actually an integral piece of life's interactive puzzle. Your unique place in the puzzle affects and influences—directly or indirectly—countless other lives.

If you feel the "beginning" of your story messed-up your contribution to the puzzle beyond repair, you are mistaken. God is in the puzzle repair business!

It is too late to have a brand-new *beginning*, but it is never too late to have a brand-new *ending*! Prepare to transform your life into one worthy of emulation.

The New You

The most important factor in your ability to live a life worth following is to recognize and accept the *new* you! This transformation occurred the instant you accepted Jesus as your personal Savior:

> Therefore, if anyone is in Christ, he *is* a new creation; old things have passed away; behold, all things have become new (2 Corinthians 5:17) (emphasis added).

Never take for granted or trivialize the uniqueness of what it means to be a follower of Jesus. To be "in Christ" is special; it is to have a personality and lifestyle dramatically different from your natural inclinations.

To avoid complacency in your Christian walk, you must understand what it means to be "in Christ." The powerful effects of your position *in Christ* will be maximized as you affirm its meaning:

In Christ, I am loved. In Christ, I am loved with a love so unimaginable as to be incomprehensible. God's love for me is so strong and binding that nothing and no one—including myself—can separate it from me (*See* Romans 8:38-39).

In Christ, I am saved. When I asked Jesus to be my personal Savior, He did so instantaneously! Not only were my sins forgiven and my guilt removed, the Holy Spirit moved into my heart to live Christ's life through me.

In Christ, I am hopeful. The Apostle Paul observed, "Christ in you, the hope of glory" (*See* Colossians 1:27). The hope of glory is no longer a mystery or simply wishful thinking. It is the confident and joyful assurance that I will someday see Jesus face to face and spend eternity in Heaven with Him.

In Christ, I am transformed. The "old" me instantly transformed into a new "baby" Christian the moment I accepted Jesus as my Savior.

Your spiritual transformation was an instantaneous miracle initiated by your *faith* in accepting Jesus Christ as your Savior. The transformation of your behavior must be initiated by conscious acts of your *will*.

As you seek a life worth following and establishing an influential legacy, consider adopting these immutable truths as your personal credo:

> *All that I am—or ever shall be—and all that I have, or ever shall have, are the direct result of God's goodness, His grace, and His mercy showered on me...and I deserve none of it!*

It All Starts in the Mind

In ancient Rome, the writing was done on a *tabula*—a slate covered with wax. Warming and smoothing-out the wax erased the writing and resulted in a *tabula rasa*—a clean slate. In philosophy, tabula rasa expresses the idea that humans are born with a "clean slate" which becomes cluttered with unlimited knowledge and life experiences.

You began life with a clean slate but by the time you became a Christian, your mind was thoroughly saturated with worldly knowledge and unhealthy influences.

Many new Christians never receive mentoring. Consequently, they suffer spiritual malnutrition and are unprepared to live a confident, godly lifestyle. Recognizing this ageless need, the Apostle Paul left this legacy:

> Do not be conformed to this world, but be transformed by the renewing of your mind, that you may prove what is that good and acceptable and perfect will of God (Romans 12:2, emphasis added).

The wheels of your mind are turning 24/7. Sometimes, your secular mind takes precedence over your Christian mind; sometimes, vice versa. Either way, your life and destiny are dramatically affected by your thoughts. In fact, your habits thus far in life have determined who you are today.

Thought patterns direct *mental* activity which determines *moral* behavior. Your thinking process must be revised before any behavioral changes can be expected. Ask your Inner Coach to guide the reprogramming of the unwise habits etched on your mind's tablet.

A Smooth Stone
You can't talk yourself out of a habit you behaved yourself into!

Transformation of thought patterns begin with a commitment to listening to and obeying God. As you study and obey His Word, your heart will become more submissive to His will and your life will become more fulfilling.

Obedience: The Master Key

Obedience is the master key to a treasure chest filled with additional life-changing keys. If you passionately believe in Jesus and desire a life worth emulating, obedience to God's expectations is the key to your future.

Utilizing the obedience key requires knowledge of God's viewpoint and His expectations as presented in the Bible. You should also be open to additional assignments delivered via *God Winks* and the guidance of your Inner Coach.

Jesus reminded His disciples that, "If you know these things, blessed are you if you do them" (John 13:17). If you want His blessings, you must remember that *knowing* and *doing* are two separate things.

When you know that you should do something and you do it, He will give you more opportunities. You may not understand an assignment, but your responsibility is to comply with God's will. Charles Stanley's advice is, "Obey God and leave all the consequences to Him."

A Smooth Stone
Don't try to figure it out...just obey Jesus!

Beware of a counterfeit of obedience! Satan will tell you God is satisfied with a few good deeds sprinkled with a pinch of self-sacrifice. He will try to convince you that reading the Bible and going to church now and then is enough for God to keep blessing you, but he is a liar!

Obedience is the key that unlocks the door of Heaven's blessings!

Personalizing Scripture will nurture a *habit of obedience* and deepen your relationship with God. This habit can be developed by frequently affirming Scripture, a conscious act that will lead to noteworthy changes in daily habits.

You may begin developing the habit of obedience by *personalizing* and speaking Bible verses to the Lord. For example:

> *I will* praise Thee, for I am fearfully and wonderfully made. Marvelous are Thy works and that my soul knows right well (Psalm 139:14, KJV, emphasis added).

> This is the day the LORD has made; *I will* rejoice and be glad in it (Psalm 118:24, emphasis added).

> God is our refuge and strength, a very present help in trouble. Therefore, *I will not* fear (Psalm 46:1-2a, emphasis added).

> In everything give thanks, for this is the will of God in Christ Jesus for *me* (1 Thessalonians 5:18, emphasis added).

> I *will* rejoice in the LORD; I *will* find joy in the God of my salvation (Habakkuk 3:18, emphasis added).

Adversity and the uncertainty of life will occasionally make obedience difficult. You may find yourself vacillating between despair and hope, doubt and faith, but you can always trust God to be faithful. He made this promise to you personally, "I will never leave you nor forsake you" (Hebrews 13:5b).

Keep your eyes focused on Jesus and your heart set on obedience and He will lead you in the absolute best ways possible!

The Key of Kindness

You are capable of showing great *compassion* or great *indifference*. These emotional responses are mutually exclusive; you must choose to nourish or suppress one or the other in individual circumstances. Which response predominates in your daily life? Compassion? Indifference? *It is your choice; choose wisely!*

During a lecture late in his life, the famous English writer, Aldous Huxley, stated, "People often ask me, 'What is the most effective technique for transforming my life?' It is a little embarrassing that after years and years of research and experimentation, I have to say that the best answer is—just be a little kinder."[4]

You were designed to be kind! When He created you in His own image, God established an escrow account of good deeds, safely set aside awaiting your attention. Long before your birth, He gently nudged the Apostle Paul to leave this message for you:

> And be kind to one another, tenderhearted, forgiving one another, even as God in Christ forgave you (Ephesians 4:32).

Kindness is a personal choice that positively influences the life of both the giver and the receiver. Genuine kindness is a composite of thoughtfulness, appreciation, generosity, respect, compassion, and humility. A gentle touch, a whisper of encouragement, a smile, an honest compliment, a listening ear are acts of kindness. An unexpected act of kindness given in the right way, at the right time is of immeasurable value, and almost anytime is the *right* time!

Acts of kindness may be as extravagant as an expensive gift or as simple as a few heartfelt words—spoken or written. Written words, in particular, carry a powerful and potentially enduring message. A handwritten (or at least personally signed) note or letter will not soon be forgotten.

Emails and text messages efficiently communicate information, but handwritten notes convey feeling and emotion directly from your heart to the recipient's heart.

Be kind to everyone. Almost everyone is burdened by some worry or personal concern. Many people struggle with emotional or physical needs that are not obvious. Be sensitive—someone wearing a smiley face on the outside may be crying on the inside.

More than two thousand years ago, the Jewish philosopher Philo counseled, "Be kind, for everyone you meet is fighting a hard battle." More recently, the renowned psychiatrist Dr. Karl Menninger underscored Philo's message with this analogy:

> *When a trout rising to a fly gets hooked and finds himself unable to swim about freely, he begins a fight which results in struggles and splashes and sometimes an escape. In the same way, the human being struggles with the hooks that catch him.*
>
> *Sometimes he masters his difficulties, sometimes they are too much for him. His struggles are all that the world sees, and it usually misunderstands them. It is hard for a free fish to understand what is happening to a hooked one.* [5]

Some people are adept at subtly keeping their real—often severe—personal concerns and needs out-of-sight. If you *assume* that everyone has at least one underlying need that a single act of kindness could alleviate... you will almost always be right! Ask your Inner Coach to increase your sensitivity to the needs of others.

Many psychologists believe that people are fundamentally more alike than different. Just as everyone needs oxygen, food, and water to survive and thrive in life, they also need frequent positive human interactions.

Make Someone's Day!

Practice taking a few minutes *every day* to make a difference in at least one person's life. Temporarily put your needs and desires aside and focus on brightening someone else's day.

Here are ten "how-to" ideas to help you make your life more others oriented:

1. *If you love someone*, tell them! Call—do not text or email—and let them hear your voice express your feelings.

2. *If you admire someone*, let them know! Write a personal note of gratitude and be specific about what you admire and appreciate about them.

3. *If you miss someone, tell them*! Make a contact personal and make their day by letting them know you are thinking about them.

4. *If you appreciate someone, make their day!* Write a personal note thanking them for just being. Then, add specifics—thank you for *being* an encourager, for *being* a good friend, for *being* a fantastic *wife*, for *being* a terrific husband and so forth.

5. *If someone needs encouragement, give it!* Most people rarely receive thoughtful and specific encouragement. Inspiring them costs you *nothing* but can mean *everything* to someone feeling sad, discouraged, or overwhelmed by life.

6. *If you can help someone, do it!* Many people are unable to take care of all their needs. Mow a lawn, take them to the grocery store or meet other physical needs.

7. *If you know someone who has lost a loved one, be there!* Unless you have first-hand experience, you cannot truly empathize but your attentiveness and encouragement, coupled with including them in your activities will bring inexpressible joy.

8. *If you know of a need, proactively meet it!* Be available to meet all kinds of needs your friends and family may encounter. If you really want to be blessed, learn about a need of someone you do not personally know and meet that need.

9. *Be an anonymous angel!* Seek and find someone's need and satisfy it

anonymously. Do not hesitate to meet a person's financial needs. You will be doubly blessed!

10. *Be an unexpected giver!* Give someone an unexpected gift. Surprise someone with a bunch of flowers, a book, or a toy on an ordinary day, i.e. not a birthday or holiday, and enjoy their excitement.

Make God's day! God will be well-pleased every time you think about and meet the needs of another of His children; He loves a cheerful giver!

What Do You Say?

Evaluate yourself. Do you have a habit of frequently speaking kind words as you go about your day-to-day activities? Your answer to these simple questions will give you a clue:

- If someone were to pay you $10 for every kind word you ever spoke, and collect $5 for every unkind word, would you be rich or poor?
- God gives you 86,400 seconds every day. How many do you use each day saying, "Thank you!"

Thoughtfully select your words. Choose to marinate conversations with *warm fuzzies* rather than *cold pricklies*! Your words can enhance or diminish another person's self-image.

Kindness is sharing yourself with someone else. Its value is incalculable and is determined by the level of need it satisfies.

The Apostle Paul communicated God's expectation for a Believer's attitude toward everyone when he wrote:

Therefore, as we have opportunity, let us do good to *all*, especially to those who are the household of faith (Galatians 6:10) (emphasis added).

A Smooth Stone
Those who do good, will do well!

Acts of kindness will satisfy the innate needs within the toughest scoundrel, the saintliest saint, and everyone in between. Everybody needs a little kindness, and the oftener it is received, the better!

We are all angels with one wing, able to fly only when we embrace each other.[6]

The Key of Gratefulness

Every human being is born with a "clean slate." Therefore, non-instinctive behavior—including gratitude—is learned behavior. A baby does not instinctively show appreciation for a clean diaper, a pacifier, or a bottle of milk.

Most children learn progressively through experience that gratefulness is a positive attribute and recognize their needs are graciously met by a source beyond themselves. Toddlers often learn to pray, "God is great, God is good, let us thank Him for our food. Amen."

As time passes, many "grow out" of childhood innocence and sub-consciously become self-centered by developing habits non-reflective of gratitude. Life being essentially binary, they evolve to being either predominately grateful or predominately non-grateful. Your philosophy on life will ultimately determine whether or not you are a grateful person.

Individuals observing the same reality can have radically different perceptions. This whimsical illustration is an excellent example of how ego or self-esteem may affect a person's attitude of appreciation:

> *A man and his wife had two pets—a dog and a cat.*
>
> *As they were sunning themselves one day, the dog said, "Our master treats me so well, he must be a king!"*
>
> *The cat yawned and purred, "Our master treats me so well, I must be a queen!"*

A grateful attitude opens the floodgates of God's delight. Have you noticed that some people have everything imaginable but live a sad and empty life while others have less than nothing and yet, enjoy a life of remarkable peace and contentment?

Henry Ward Beecher, the nineteenth-century American preacher employed wonderful imagery to illustrate the distinction between grateful and ungrateful people.

> *"Suppose someone gave you a dish of sand mixed with fine iron filings. You look for the filings with your eyes; you comb for them with your fingers. But you can't find them.*
>
> *Then, you take a tiny magnet and draw it throughout the dish. Suddenly, the magnet is covered with iron filings.*
>
> *The ungrateful person is like our hands combing the sand. Such a person finds nothing to be thankful for. The grateful person, on the other hand, is like the magnet sweeping throughout the sand, and finding hundreds of things to be thankful for."*

Like a magnet, a grateful mindset is attracted to God's blessings—great and small. Are your thoughts constantly focused on negative feelings or do they attract the positive "iron filings" of God's blessings? A grateful mindset is a personal choice. *Choose it!*

A Smooth Stone
An attitude of gratitude should flavor everything you do!

Since you began life with nothing and now have something—and lots of it—what should be the logical response to whoever made it possible?

A thoughtful expression of appreciation will be a blessing that strengthens and deepens the relationship.

Failure to express gratitude is like receiving a gift and never unwrapping it.

The unintended message is that the gift—and its giver—are unimportant. *You really do* appreciate their thoughtfulness, time, and effort but you just never got around to thanking them.

> He was conscripted into service on June 26, 1944. Eight months later, forty-four-year-old Egawa Masaharu was performing the unfamiliar duties of a Japanese Army platoon leader on Iwo Jima. A few days prior to the invasion of the island by United States Marines on February 19, 1945, Egawa wrote a final letter to his wife, Mitsue:

There were many occasions when I should have expressed my gratitude to you—I had the means to do so after all—but I thought that the feeling of gratitude within me was enough by itself, so I did not make the effort to say "Thank you." It is something I regret deeply. Do not think badly of me. I hope you will forgive me.[7]

On or before March 26, 1945, Egawa died in battle; Mitsue became a widow and two daughters became fatherless.

A Smooth Stone
Unexpressed gratitude appears to be ingratitude!

Why is expressing gratitude important? Ask yourself: "What positive characteristics or possessions do I have that were not given to me?" After giving it serious thought and a bit of rationalization, your conclusion will undoubtedly be, "*Nothing!*"

> *Every* good gift and *every* perfect gift is from above, and comes down from the Father of lights, with whom there is no variation or shadow of turning (James 1:17) (emphasis added).

When you become so proud as to believe you are responsible for your accomplishments, forget it! There are no "self-made" men or women. Here is the fact of the matter:

> And you shall remember the LORD your God, for it is He who gives you the power to get wealth (Deuteronomy 8:18a).

The attitudes you *choose* and the choices you make reflect not only the quality of your life but also how you express gratefulness. Choosing obedience to God will result in behavior expressing appreciation and thankfulness. His desire for you on is crystal clear:

> In *everything* give thanks for this is the will of God in Christ Jesus for you (1 Thessalonians 5:18, emphasis added).

Cultivating a consistent attitude of gratitude may require a commitment to making personal changes. Four suggestions to help you overcome behavior that inhibits gratitude:

1. *Develop positive thought patterns.* Negativity and pessimism are antithetical to gratitude. *See* Philippians 4:4-9.

2. *Count your blessings early and often.* Don't forget to count the blessings disguised as disappointments.

3. *Make a personal vow to practice gratitude.* Write this promise to yourself: "I will choose an attitude of gratitude at all times." And keep it close by so you will see it often.

4. *Think outside the box.* Acknowledge that many bad breaks, disappointments, and difficult circumstances which seem bad at the time will later prove to be in your best interests. *See* Romans 8:28.

Every experience contains the seeds of blessing and lessons to be learned. A grateful attitude ensures that a positive response in situations beyond your control will result in deepening your relationship with God.

After being robbed, the eminent 17th Century preacher Matthew Henry prayed, "I thank Thee first, because I was never robbed before, second, because although they took my purse, they did not take my life; third, because although they took my all, it was not much; and fourth, because it was I who was robbed, and not I who robbed.

A grateful attitude is important in any relationship but *is absolutely essential* to a meaningful relationship with God. How can we express gratitude to God? What gift can we offer Him that He has not previously given us?

Our obedience and expressions of gratitude are the *only* gifts we can give God that He has not given us. He gave us the *ability* to be grateful, but we must choose to activate that ability within our relationships.

Gratefulness is a gift that keeps on giving! An attitude of gratitude can ignite a perpetual cycle of goodness:

- Gratitude sparks generosity.
- Generosity leads to blessings.
- Blessings promote gratitude...and the cycle repeats.

Gratitude is an attitude that determines the ways you express gratefulness to God and to others. The attitude you *choose* toward life's unpredictable circumstances reveal not only to the quality of your life but your commitment to express gratitude in "all things."

Four Action Items

Developing a continuous attitude of gratitude may require relatively minor changes to your daily routine. Consider implementing these suggestions to your daily activities:

Take time to be grateful! You can only be thankful for the things you notice and enjoy. Become a noticer! Learn to appreciate the insignificant things in life and make this your personal prayer:

"Lord, help me appreciate what I *have*
before time forces me to appreciate what I *had*!"

Create a Me File! When sadness or disappointment leads to discouragement, pause and become reflective. Think about a time you were blessed by a visit, a phone call or personal note, a greeting card or a photograph. Keep these memorabilia readily available in a *"Me File"* placed in a folder, box, or desk drawer...you will be glad you did!

Launch a 3:16 Routine! Schedule a notification on your cell phone for 3:16 p.m. every day as a reminder to praise God. *He is worthy of your praise—and then some!* Make a habit of thanking and praising Him at the same time every day through meditation of the Scripture: For example:

> For God so loved the world that He gave his only begotten Son, that whoever believes in Him should not perish but have everlasting life (John 3:16).

> I will praise You, for I am fearfully and wonderfully made; marvelous are Your works and that my soul knows very well (Psalm 139:14).

Keep a Gratitude Journal: A wise old philosopher once observed, "The palest ink is better than the best memory." A Gratitude Journal will help you avoid the sin of taking God's blessings for granted.

Establish a practice of daily recalling moments of gratitude, blessings, and memories that have special value and meaning to you. Someday you will view them as "precious memories."

Chapter Notes

1. William James (1842–1910) was an American philosopher and psychologist.

2. Ethel Waters (1896–1977) was an American singer and actress.

3. Dr. Orison Swett Marden (1848–1924) was an American inspirational author who wrote about achieving success in life and founded *SUCCESS* magazine in 1897. His writings discuss common-sense principles and virtues

that make for a well-rounded, successful life.

4. Aldous Huxley (1894–1963) was an English writer and philosopher; the author of *Brave New World*. This quote is from a lecture published in *The Power of Kindness* by Piero Ferrucci (New York: Penguin Group, 2006) p. 8.

5. Dr. Karl Menninger (1893–1990) was an American psychiatrist. Quote is from his book, *The Human Mind*, (New York: Alfred A. Knopf, 1945).

6. Mark Albion, American author as quoted in the premiere issue (2006) of *Motto* magazine.

7. Information source: *So Sad to Fall in Battle* by Kumiko Kakehashi, copyright © 2005 by Kumiko Kakehashi. Translation copyright © 2007 by Shinchosha Co., Ltd. Tokyo,

Chapter 13
The Gratitude Journal

You never know the value of a moment
until it becomes a memory.
—Dr. Seuss[1]

Life is full of beginnings...every hour, every day.

Most beginnings are exceedingly small. One raindrop is the genesis of a flood. One acorn produces a towering oak tree. One spark from a campfire ignites a forest fire and one small idea can revolutionize your life!

One small idea can stimulate life-changing behavior. An idea like learning to pay attention and take appropriate action in the present moment. Or an idea to *postpone procrastination* while developing habits that spark a continuous attitude of gratitude. The habit of keeping a gratitude journal offers this life-changing opportunity.

Unfortunately—as Dr. Seuss suggests—we sometimes fail to appreciate the beauty and significance of life's "little things" until we see them through the lens of 20/20 hindsight. Looking back, it is obvious our tacit authorization of unwise and/or misplaced priorities unduly affected our life.

The problem is we allow the vortex of 21st Century busyness to inordinately influence our decisions. A frenetic pace of life can strain relationships and cast a cloud over dreams of the future. It can cause disappointment and discouragement that suck the joy out of life.

A solution worth considering is developing the habit of stepping aside from life's pressures and drawing close to God for a few minutes. Relax. Catch your breath. Pay attention to and enjoy the seemingly insignificant things happening around you: a fluttering butterfly, the soft patter of rainfall, a child's giggle. *Praise God for all the goodness you see and enjoy!*

Have you begun the habit of praising God at 3:16 p.m. every day? If so, your focus is on keeping *the main thing the main thing*. Another helpful habit is to have a regimen for organizing thoughts into memories.

The exercise of writing about people, events, and blessings is an invaluable investment. This process helps keep life in perspective and enables you to capitalize on the full value of its experiences.

A fifty-two-week *Gratitude Journal* to serve as a repository of memories, thoughts, self-reflection, and a record of faithfulness in expressing gratitude follows this chapter. Its design layout will prompt you to pay attention to God, to others and to yourself.

Make God's Day!

Few things—I suspect—please God more than a Christian memorizing His Word and leaning on its wisdom each day. Marinating a verse in your mind naturally leads to praise... and that will make His day!

The Bible is the most useful navigational aid available for transitioning to a life worth emulating. Each weekly page contains a personal message from God giving wisdom and strength for the daily grind.

Memorizing God's Word gives instant access to its therapeutic power. Charles L. Allen[2] often wrote this "prescription" for those whom he counseled:

> *Read the 23rd Psalm five times daily for seven days. Read it thoroughly and unhurriedly first thing upon getting up in the morning, immediately after breakfast, after lunch, after dinner, and just before going to bed.*

The amazing results obtained by those following his advice underscores the therapeutic value of meditating on Scripture. You will be wise to accept the healing nourishment available in God's Word!

Memorize the weekly Bible verse! The power in memorizing Scripture does not reside in your ability to remember and recite the words. The amazing, unlimited power of God's Word becomes readily available as your mind synchronizes with the mind of God.

An investment in memorizing Bible verses pays enormous dividends. Adversity will inevitably come your way, but you will be well-prepared when it arrives.

A Smooth Stone
When the time of need arrives, the time for preparation has passed.

Think about and document specific blessings from God on the lines within your Gratitude Journal. You will not need to look far and wide to fill-in these blanks...blessings are everywhere! A worthwhile initial entry each week is, "*I have memorized this week's Bible verse!*"

Make Someone's Day!

With one trifling exception, the entire population of the world is comprised of other people. Surely, you can find *someone* in that crowd to bless with a thoughtful and unexpected gift of kindness!

Take a few minutes each week to make a difference in another person's life. Set aside your needs and desires and focus on brightening someone else's day. There are many ways to uplift their spirits and bring them joy and happiness. Here are two ideas from a longer list in Chapter Twelve:

> *Be an anonymous angel!* Seek and find someone's need and satisfy it anonymously. Do not hesitate to meet a person's financial needs; you will be doubly blessed!

> *Be an unexpected giver!* Give someone an unexpected gift. Surprise someone with a bunch of flowers, a book, or a toy on an ordinary day, i.e. not a birthday or holiday and then enjoy their excitement!

A Smooth Stone
Be kind to unkind people; they are the ones who need it most.

Remember—when you make someone else's day, you are also making God's day! *He loves a thoughtful, cheerful giver!*

Make Your Day!

The more memories you have, the more "you" you have!

Make a special effort to remember and relive wonderful memories from yesterday or the more distant past. You will discover that as you draw upon one memory, a linkage to another will come to mind. Write them down...you will be glad you did!

Entries with names, places, and dates are substantially more meaningful. Don't overlook writing about the hardship and adversity you have overcome. Every victory—large and small—can be an encouragement in the days ahead.

Begin Today!

Keep your entries positive and upbeat. Positive, optimistic, and loving thoughts and remembrances seem to release "feel good" neurotransmitters in the brain—and who doesn't want to feel good!

Create each entry with zest and enthusiasm by using words like happy, excited, elated, amazed, loved, adored, cherished, supportive, fussed-over, honored, joyful, delighted, glad, grateful, overjoyed, thrilled, carefree, unworthy, gratified, ecstatic and pleased.

You will occasionally be reminded of a conversation, event, or other experience when your journal is not readily available. Make note of the memory—on your hand, if necessary—until you can precisely record it in your journal.

And now...let the journaling begin!

Chapter Notes

1. Theodor Seuss Geisel (1904–1991) was an American children's author, political cartoonist, and illustrator. He is well-known for writing and illustrating more than 60 books under the pen name *Dr. Seuss*.

2. Charles L. Allen (1913–2005) was an American Methodist minister, pastor, and author. This illustration is from his book, *The Twenty-Third Psalm, An Interpretation* (Westwood, NJ: Fleming H. Revell Company, 1961) pp. 11-13.

My
Gratitude
Journal

My Gratitude Journal

Trust in the Lord with all your heart and lean not on your own
understanding; in all your ways acknowledge Him,
and He shall direct your paths.
—Proverbs 3:5–6

Make God's Day!
(What can you praise God for today?)

1. _____
2. _____
3. _____
4. _____
5. _____
6. _____
7. _____

Make Someone's Day!
(Be an encourager or a blessing to someone!)

1. _____
2. _____
3. _____
4. _____
5. _____

Make Your Day!
(Create and enjoy memories!)

1. _____
2. _____
3. _____
4. _____
5. _____

(Remember to include names, dates, and places.)

Week 1

My Gratitude Journal

Rejoice always, pray without ceasing,
in everything give thanks,
for this is the will of God in Christ Jesus for you.
—1 Thessalonians 5:16–18

Make God's Day!
(What can you praise God for today?)

1. _____
2. _____
3. _____
4. _____
5. _____
6. _____
7. _____

Make Someone's Day!
(Be an encourager or a blessing to someone!)

1. _____
2. _____
3. _____
4. _____
5. _____

Make Your Day!
(Create and enjoy memories!)

1. _____
2. _____
3. _____
4. _____
5. _____

(Remember to include names, dates, and places.)

Week 2

My Gratitude Journal

He has shown you, O man, what is good;
And what does the LORD require of you but to do justly,
to love mercy, and to walk humbly with your God?
—Micah 6:8

Make God's Day!
(What can you praise God for today?)

1. _____
2. _____
3. _____
4. _____
5. _____
6. _____
7. _____

Make Someone's Day!
(Be an encourager or a blessing to someone!)

1. _____
2. _____
3. _____
4. _____
5. _____

Make Your Day!
(Create and enjoy memories!)

1. _____
2. _____
3. _____
4. _____
5. _____

(Remember to include names, dates, and places.)

Week 3

My Gratitude Journal

Commit your works to the LORD,
and your thoughts will be established.
—Proverbs 16:3

Make God's Day!
(What can you praise God for today?)

1. _____
2. _____
3. _____
4. _____
5. _____
6. _____
7. _____

Make Someone's Day!
(Be an encourager or a blessing to someone!)

1. _____
2. _____
3. _____
4. _____
5. _____

Make Your Day!
(Create and enjoy memories!)

1. _____
2. _____
3. _____
4. _____
5. _____

(Remember to include names, dates, and places.)

Week 4

My Gratitude Journal

I will praise You,
for I am fearfully and wonderfully made;
Marvelous are Your works and that my soul knows very well.
—Psalm 139:14

Make God's Day!
(What can you praise God for today?)

1. _____
2. _____
3. _____
4. _____
5. _____
6. _____
7. _____

Make Someone's Day!
(Be an encourager or a blessing to someone!)

1. _____
2. _____
3. _____
4. _____
5. _____

Make Your Day!
(Create and enjoy memories!)

1. _____
2. _____
3. _____
4. _____
5. _____

(Remember to include names, dates, and places.)

Week 5

My Gratitude Journal

Show me the right path, O LORD; point out the road for me to follow.
Lead me by Your truth and teach me, for You are the God who saves me.
All day long I put my hope in You.
—Psalm 25:4–5 (NLT)

Make God's Day!
(What can you praise God for today?)

1. _____
2. _____
3. _____
4. _____
5. _____
6. _____
7. _____

Make Someone's Day!
(Be an encourager or a blessing to someone!)

1. _____
2. _____
3. _____
4. _____
5. _____

Make Your Day!
(Create and enjoy memories!)

1. _____
2. _____
3. _____
4. _____
5. _____

(Remember to include names, dates, and places.)

Week 6

My Gratitude Journal

And be kind to one another,
tenderhearted, forgiving one another,
even as God in Christ forgave you.
—Ephesians 4:32

Make God's Day!
(What can you praise God for today?)

1. _____
2. _____
3. _____
4. _____
5. _____
6. _____
7. _____

Make Someone's Day!
(Be an encourager or a blessing to someone!)

1. _____
2. _____
3. _____
4. _____
5. _____

Make Your Day!
(Create and enjoy memories!)

1. _____
2. _____
3. _____
4. _____
5. _____

(Remember to include names, dates, and places.)

Week 7

My Gratitude Journal

But be doers of the word,
and not hearers only,
deceiving yourselves.
—James 1:22

Make God's Day!
(What can you praise God for today?)

1. _____
2. _____
3. _____
4. _____
5. _____
6. _____
7. _____

Make Someone's Day!
(Be an encourager or a blessing to someone!)

1. _____
2. _____
3. _____
4. _____
5. _____

Make Your Day!
(Create and enjoy memories!)

1. _____
2. _____
3. _____
4. _____
5. _____

(Remember to include names, dates, and places.)

Week 8

My Gratitude Journal

Do not be deceived, God is not mocked;
for whatever a man sows, that he will also reap.
—Galatians 6:7

Make God's Day!
(What can you praise God for today?)

1. _____
2. _____
3. _____
4. _____
5. _____
6. _____
7. _____

Make Someone's Day!
(Be an encourager or a blessing to someone!)

1. _____
2. _____
3. _____
4. _____
5. _____

Make Your Day!
(Create and enjoy memories!)

1. _____
2. _____
3. _____
4. _____
5. _____

(Remember to include names, dates, and places.)

Week 9

My Gratitude Journal

In the morning sow your seed, and in the evening do not
withhold your hand; for you do not know which will prosper,
either this or that, or whether both alike will be good.
—Ecclesiastes 11:6

Make God's Day!
(What can you praise God for today?)

1. _____
2. _____
3. _____
4. _____
5. _____
6. _____
7. _____

Make Someone's Day!
(Be an encourager or a blessing to someone!)

1. _____
2. _____
3. _____
4. _____
5. _____

Make Your Day!
(Create and enjoy memories!)

1. _____
2. _____
3. _____
4. _____
5. _____

(Remember to include names, dates, and places.)

Week 10

My Gratitude Journal

And my God shall supply all your need
according to His riches in glory in Christ Jesus.
—Philippians 4:19

Make God's Day!
(What can you praise God for today?)

1. _____
2. _____
3. _____
4. _____
5. _____
6. _____
7. _____

Make Someone's Day!
(Be an encourager or a blessing to someone!)

1. _____
2. _____
3. _____
4. _____
5. _____

Make Your Day!
(Create and enjoy memories!)

1. _____
2. _____
3. _____
4. _____
5. _____

(Remember to include names, dates, and places.)

Week 11

My Gratitude Journal

Call unto me, and I will answer you,
and show you great and mighty things,
which you do not know.
—Jeremiah 33:3

Make God's Day!
(What can you praise God for today?)

1. _____
2. _____
3. _____
4. _____
5. _____
6. _____
7. _____

Make Someone's Day!
(Be an encourager or a blessing to someone!)

1. _____
2. _____
3. _____
4. _____
5. _____

Make Your Day!
(Create and enjoy memories!)

1. _____
2. _____
3. _____
4. _____
5. _____

(Remember to include names, dates, and places.)

Week 12

My Gratitude Journal

When a man's ways please the LORD,
He makes even his enemies to be at peace with him.
—Proverbs 16:7

Make God's Day!
(What can you praise God for today?)

1. _____
2. _____
3. _____
4. _____
5. _____
6. _____
7. _____

Make Someone's Day!
(Be an encourager or a blessing to someone!)

1. _____
2. _____
3. _____
4. _____
5. _____

Make Your Day!
(Create and enjoy memories!)

1. _____
2. _____
3. _____
4. _____
5. _____

(Remember to include names, dates, and places.)

Week 13

My Gratitude Journal

When you make a vow to God, do not delay to fulfill it.
He has no pleasure in fools; fulfill your vow.
It is better not to make a vow than to make one and not fulfill it.
—Ecclesiastes 5:4–5 (NIV)

Make God's Day!
(What can you praise God for today?)

1. _____
2. _____
3. _____
4. _____
5. _____
6. _____
7. _____

Make Someone's Day!
(Be an encourager or a blessing to someone!)

1. _____
2. _____
3. _____
4. _____
5. _____

Make Your Day!
(Create and enjoy memories!)

1. _____
2. _____
3. _____
4. _____
5. _____

(Remember to include names, dates, and places.)

Week 14

My Gratitude Journal

If any of you lacks wisdom, let him ask of God, who gives
to all liberally and without reproach,
and it will be given to him.
—James 1:5

Make God's Day!
(What can you praise God for today?)

1. _____
2. _____
3. _____
4. _____
5. _____
6. _____
7. _____

Make Someone's Day!
(Be an encourager or a blessing to someone!)

1. _____
2. _____
3. _____
4. _____
5. _____

Make Your Day!
(Create and enjoy memories!)

1. _____
2. _____
3. _____
4. _____
5. _____

(Remember to include names, dates, and places.)

Week 15

My Gratitude Journal

For I consider that the sufferings of this present time
are not worthy to be compared with
the glory which shall be revealed in us.
—Romans 8:18

Make God's Day!
(What can you praise God for today?)

1. _____
2. _____
3. _____
4. _____
5. _____
6. _____
7. _____

Make Someone's Day!
(Be an encourager or a blessing to someone!)

1. _____
2. _____
3. _____
4. _____
5. _____

Make Your Day!
(Create and enjoy memories!)

1. _____
2. _____
3. _____
4. _____
5. _____

(Remember to include names, dates, and places.)

Week 16

My Gratitude Journal

Let another man praise you,
and not your own mouth;
A stranger, and not your own lips.
—Proverbs 27:2

Make God's Day!
(What can you praise God for today?)

1. _____
2. _____
3. _____
4. _____
5. _____
6. _____
7. _____

Make Someone's Day!
(Be an encourager or a blessing to someone!)

1. _____
2. _____
3. _____
4. _____
5. _____

Make Your Day!
(Create and enjoy memories!)

1. _____
2. _____
3. _____
4. _____
5. _____

(Remember to include names, dates, and places.)

Week 17

My Gratitude Journal

In My Father's house are many mansions;
if it were not so, I would have told you.
I go to prepare a place for you.
—John 14:2

Make God's Day!
(What can you praise God for today?)

1. _____
2. _____
3. _____
4. _____
5. _____
6. _____
7. _____

Make Someone's Day!
(Be an encourager or a blessing to someone!)

1. _____
2. _____
3. _____
4. _____
5. _____

Make Your Day!
(Create and enjoy memories!)

1. _____
2. _____
3. _____
4. _____
5. _____

(Remember to include names, dates, and places.)

Week 18

My Gratitude Journal

And if I go and prepare a place for you,
I will come again and receive you to Myself;
that where I am, there you may be also.
—John 14:3

Make God's Day!
(What can you praise God for today?)

1. _____
2. _____
3. _____
4. _____
5. _____
6. _____
7. _____

Make Someone's Day!
(Be an encourager or a blessing to someone!)

1. _____
2. _____
3. _____
4. _____
5. _____

Make Your Day!
(Create and enjoy memories!)

1. _____
2. _____
3. _____
4. _____
5. _____

(Remember to include names, dates, and places.)

Week 19

My Gratitude Journal

And you shall remember
the LORD your God, for it is He
who gives you the power to get wealth.
—Deuteronomy 8:18b

Make God's Day!
(What can you praise God for today?)

1. _____
2. _____
3. _____
4. _____
5. _____
6. _____
7. _____

Make Someone's Day!
(Be an encourager or a blessing to someone!)

1. _____
2. _____
3. _____
4. _____
5. _____

Make Your Day!
(Create and enjoy memories!)

1. _____
2. _____
3. _____
4. _____
5. _____

(Remember to include names, dates, and places.)

Week 20

My Gratitude Journal

And you shall love the LORD your God
with all your heart, with all your soul,
with all your mind, and with all your strength.
—Mark 12:30a

Make God's Day!
(What can you praise God for today?)

1. _____
2. _____
3. _____
4. _____
5. _____
6. _____
7. _____

Make Someone's Day!
(Be an encourager or a blessing to someone!)

1. _____
2. _____
3. _____
4. _____
5. _____

Make Your Day!
(Create and enjoy memories!)

1. _____
2. _____
3. _____
4. _____
5. _____

(Remember to include names, dates, and places.)

Week 21

My Gratitude Journal

The steps of a good man
are ordered by the LORD,
and He delights in his way.
—Psalm 37:23

Make God's Day!
(What can you praise God for today?)

1. _____
2. _____
3. _____
4. _____
5. _____
6. _____
7. _____

Make Someone's Day!
(Be an encourager or a blessing to someone!)

1. _____
2. _____
3. _____
4. _____
5. _____

Make Your Day!
(Create and enjoy memories!)

1. _____
2. _____
3. _____
4. _____
5. _____

(Remember to include names, dates, and places.)

Week 22

My Gratitude Journal

Humble yourselves
in the sight of the Lord,
and He will lift you up.
—James 4:10

Make God's Day!
(What can you praise God for today?)

1. _____
2. _____
3. _____
4. _____
5. _____
6. _____
7. _____

Make Someone's Day!
(Be an encourager or a blessing to someone!)

1. _____
2. _____
3. _____
4. _____
5. _____

Make Your Day!
(Create and enjoy memories!)

1. _____
2. _____
3. _____
4. _____
5. _____

(Remember to include names, dates, and places.)

Week 23

My Gratitude Journal

Whoever sows sparingly will also reap sparingly,
and whoever sows generously
will also reap generously.
—2 Corinthians 9:6b

Make God's Day!
(What can you praise God for today?)

1. _____
2. _____
3. _____
4. _____
5. _____
6. _____
7. _____

Make Someone's Day!
(Be an encourager or a blessing to someone!)

1. _____
2. _____
3. _____
4. _____
5. _____

Make Your Day!
(Create and enjoy memories!)

1. _____
2. _____
3. _____
4. _____
5. _____

(Remember to include names, dates, and places.)

Week 24

My Gratitude Journal

You will keep him in perfect peace,
whose mind is stayed on You,
because he trusts in You.
—Isaiah 26:3

Make God's Day!
(What can you praise God for today?)

1. _____
2. _____
3. _____
4. _____
5. _____
6. _____
7. _____

Make Someone's Day!
(Be an encourager or a blessing to someone!)

1. _____
2. _____
3. _____
4. _____
5. _____

Make Your Day!
(Create and enjoy memories!)

1. _____
2. _____
3. _____
4. _____
5. _____

(Remember to include names, dates, and places.)

Week 25

My Gratitude Journal

For the eyes of the LORD are on the righteous,
And His ears are open to their prayers;
But the face of the Lord is against those who do evil.
—1 Peter 3:12

Make God's Day!
(What can you praise God for today?)

1. _____
2. _____
3. _____
4. _____
5. _____
6. _____
7. _____

Make Someone's Day!
(Be an encourager or a blessing to someone!)

1. _____
2. _____
3. _____
4. _____
5. _____

Make Your Day!
(Create and enjoy memories!)

1. _____
2. _____
3. _____
4. _____
5. _____

(Remember to include names, dates, and places.)

Week 26

My Gratitude Journal

For I know whom I have believed and am persuaded
that He is able to keep what I have committed
to Him until that Day.
—2 Timothy 1:12b

Make God's Day!
(What can you praise God for today?)

1. _____
2. _____
3. _____
4. _____
5. _____
6. _____
7. _____

Make Someone's Day!
(Be an encourager or a blessing to someone!)

1. _____
2. _____
3. _____
4. _____
5. _____

Make Your Day!
(Create and enjoy memories!)

1. _____
2. _____
3. _____
4. _____
5. _____

(Remember to include names, dates, and places.)

Week 27

My Gratitude Journal

Jesus said to him,
"I am the way, the truth, and the life.
No one comes to the Father except through Me."
—John 14:6

Make God's Day!
(What can you praise God for today?)

1. _____
2. _____
3. _____
4. _____
5. _____
6. _____
7. _____

Make Someone's Day!
(Be an encourager or a blessing to someone!)

1. _____
2. _____
3. _____
4. _____
5. _____

Make Your Day!
(Create and enjoy memories!)

1. _____
2. _____
3. _____
4. _____
5. _____

(Remember to include names, dates, and places.)

Week 28

My Gratitude Journal

I sought the LORD,
and He heard me, and
delivered me from all my fears.
—Psalm 34:4

Make God's Day!
(What can you praise God for today?)

1. _____
2. _____
3. _____
4. _____
5. _____
6. _____
7. _____

Make Someone's Day!
(Be an encourager or a blessing to someone!)

1. _____
2. _____
3. _____
4. _____
5. _____

Make Your Day!
(Create and enjoy memories!)

1. _____
2. _____
3. _____
4. _____
5. _____

(Remember to include names, dates, and places.)

Week 29

My Gratitude Journal

A word fitly spoken
is like apples of gold
in settings of silver.
—Proverbs 25:11

Make God's Day!
(What can you praise God for today?)

1. _____
2. _____
3. _____
4. _____
5. _____
6. _____
7. _____

Make Someone's Day!
(Be an encourager or a blessing to someone!)

1. _____
2. _____
3. _____
4. _____
5. _____

Make Your Day!
(Create and enjoy memories!)

1. _____
2. _____
3. _____
4. _____
5. _____

(Remember to include names, dates, and places.)

Week 30

My Gratitude Journal

For I am not ashamed of the gospel of Christ,
for it is the power of God to salvation
for everyone who believes.
—Romans 1:16a

Make God's Day!
(What can you praise God for today?)

1. _____
2. _____
3. _____
4. _____
5. _____
6. _____
7. _____

Make Someone's Day!
(Be an encourager or a blessing to someone!)

1. _____
2. _____
3. _____
4. _____
5. _____

Make Your Day!
(Create and enjoy memories!)

1. _____
2. _____
3. _____
4. _____
5. _____

(Remember to include names, dates, and places.)

Week 31

My Gratitude Journal

I have been crucified with Christ; it is no longer I who live,
but Christ lives in me; and the life which I now live in the flesh
I live by faith in the Son of God, who loved me and gave Himself for me.
—Galatians 2:20

Make God's Day!
(What can you praise God for today?)

1. _____
2. _____
3. _____
4. _____
5. _____
6. _____
7. _____

Make Someone's Day!
(Be an encourager or a blessing to someone!)

1. _____
2. _____
3. _____
4. _____
5. _____

Make Your Day!
(Create and enjoy memories!)

1. _____
2. _____
3. _____
4. _____
5. _____

(Remember to include names, dates, and places.)

Week 32

My Gratitude Journal

Be still and know that I am God;
I will be exalted among the nations,
I will be exalted in the earth!
—Psalm 46:10

Make God's Day!
(What can you praise God for today?)

1. _____
2. _____
3. _____
4. _____
5. _____
6. _____
7. _____

Make Someone's Day!
(Be an encourager or a blessing to someone!)

1. _____
2. _____
3. _____
4. _____
5. _____

Make Your Day!
(Create and enjoy memories!)

1. _____
2. _____
3. _____
4. _____
5. _____

(Remember to include names, dates, and places.)

Week 33

My Gratitude Journal

For God so loved the world that He gave His only begotten Son,
that whoever believes in Him
should not perish but have everlasting life.
—John 3:16

Make God's Day!
(What can you praise God for today?)

1. _____
2. _____
3. _____
4. _____
5. _____
6. _____
7. _____

Make Someone's Day!
(Be an encourager or a blessing to someone!)

1. _____
2. _____
3. _____
4. _____
5. _____

Make Your Day!
(Create and enjoy memories!)

1. _____
2. _____
3. _____
4. _____
5. _____

(Remember to include names, dates, and places.)

Week 34

My Gratitude Journal

Eye has not seen, nor ear heard,
nor have entered into the heart of man
the things which God has prepared for those who love Him.
—1 Corinthians 2:9b

Make God's Day!
(What can you praise God for today?)

1. _____
2. _____
3. _____
4. _____
5. _____
6. _____
7. _____

Make Someone's Day!
(Be an encourager or a blessing to someone!)

1. _____
2. _____
3. _____
4. _____
5. _____

Make Your Day!
(Create and enjoy memories!)

1. _____
2. _____
3. _____
4. _____
5. _____

(Remember to include names, dates, and places.)

Week 35

My Gratitude Journal

But without faith it is impossible to please Him,
for he who comes to God must believe that He is, and that
He is a rewarder of those who diligently seek Him.
—Hebrews 11:6

Make God's Day!
(What can you praise God for today?)

1. _____
2. _____
3. _____
4. _____
5. _____
6. _____
7. _____

Make Someone's Day!
(Be an encourager or a blessing to someone!)

1. _____
2. _____
3. _____
4. _____
5. _____

Make Your Day!
(Create and enjoy memories!)

1. _____
2. _____
3. _____
4. _____
5. _____

(Remember to include names, dates, and places.)

Week 36

My Gratitude Journal

If then you were raised with Christ,
seek those things which are above, where Christ is,
sitting at the right hand of God.
—Colossians 3:1

Make God's Day!
(What can you praise God for today?)

1. _____
2. _____
3. _____
4. _____
5. _____
6. _____
7. _____

Make Someone's Day!
(Be an encourager or a blessing to someone!)

1. _____
2. _____
3. _____
4. _____
5. _____

Make Your Day!
(Create and enjoy memories!)

1. _____
2. _____
3. _____
4. _____
5. _____

(Remember to include names, dates, and places.)

Week 37

My Gratitude Journal

All hard work brings a profit,
but mere talk
leads only to poverty.
—Proverbs 14:23 (NIV)

Make God's Day!
(What can you praise God for today?)

1. _____
2. _____
3. _____
4. _____
5. _____
6. _____
7. _____

Make Someone's Day!
(Be an encourager or a blessing to someone!)

1. _____
2. _____
3. _____
4. _____
5. _____

Make Your Day!
(Create and enjoy memories!)

1. _____
2. _____
3. _____
4. _____
5. _____

(Remember to include names, dates, and places.)

Week 38

My Gratitude Journal

And my God shall supply all your need
according to His riches in glory
by Christ Jesus.
—Philippians 4:19

Make God's Day!
(What can you praise God for today?)

1. _____
2. _____
3. _____
4. _____
5. _____
6. _____
7. _____

Make Someone's Day!
(Be an encourager or a blessing to someone!)

1. _____
2. _____
3. _____
4. _____
5. _____

Make Your Day!
(Create and enjoy memories!)

1. _____
2. _____
3. _____
4. _____
5. _____

(Remember to include names, dates, and places.)

Week 39

My Gratitude Journal

And whatever you do in word or deed,
do all in the name of the Lord Jesus,
giving thanks to God the Father through Him.
—Colossians 3:17

Make God's Day!
(What can you praise God for today?)

1. _____
2. _____
3. _____
4. _____
5. _____
6. _____
7. _____

Make Someone's Day!
(Be an encourager or a blessing to someone!)

1. _____
2. _____
3. _____
4. _____
5. _____

Make Your Day!
(Create and enjoy memories!)

1. _____
2. _____
3. _____
4. _____
5. _____

(Remember to include names, dates, and places.)

Week 40

My Gratitude Journal

So humble yourselves under the mighty power of God,
and at the right time, He will lift you up in honor.
Give all your worries and cares to God, for He cares about you.
—1 Peter 5:6-7 (NLT)

Make God's Day!
(What can you praise God for today?)

1. _____
2. _____
3. _____
4. _____
5. _____
6. _____
7. _____

Make Someone's Day!
(Be an encourager or a blessing to someone!)

1. _____
2. _____
3. _____
4. _____
5. _____

Make Your Day!
(Create and enjoy memories!)

1. _____
2. _____
3. _____
4. _____
5. _____

(Remember to include names, dates, and places.)

Week 41

My Gratitude Journal

Therefore submit to God.
Resist the devil and he will flee from you.
Draw near to God and He will draw near to you.
—James 4:7–8a

Make God's Day!
(What can you praise God for today?)

1. _____
2. _____
3. _____
4. _____
5. _____
6. _____
7. _____

Make Someone's Day!
(Be an encourager or a blessing to someone!)

1. _____
2. _____
3. _____
4. _____
5. _____

Make Your Day!
(Create and enjoy memories!)

1. _____
2. _____
3. _____
4. _____
5. _____

(Remember to include names, dates, and places.)

Week 42

My Gratitude Journal

Bear one another's burdens, and so fulfill the law of Christ.
For if anyone thinks himself to be something,
when he is nothing, he deceives himself.
—Galatians 6:2–3

Make God's Day!
(What can you praise God for today?)

1. _____
2. _____
3. _____
4. _____
5. _____
6. _____
7. _____

Make Someone's Day!
(Be an encourager or a blessing to someone!)

1. _____
2. _____
3. _____
4. _____
5. _____

Make Your Day!
(Create and enjoy memories!)

1. _____
2. _____
3. _____
4. _____
5. _____

(Remember to include names, dates, and places.)

Week 43

My Gratitude Journal

Great peace have those who love Your law,
and nothing causes them to stumble.
—Psalm 119:165

Make God's Day!
(What can you praise God for today?)

1. _____
2. _____
3. _____
4. _____
5. _____
6. _____
7. _____

Make Someone's Day!
(Be an encourager or a blessing to someone!)

1. _____
2. _____
3. _____
4. _____
5. _____

Make Your Day!
(Create and enjoy memories!)

1. _____
2. _____
3. _____
4. _____
5. _____

(Remember to include names, dates, and places.)

Week 44

My Gratitude Journal

If you confess with your mouth the Lord Jesus and
believe in your heart that God has raised Him from the dead,
you will be saved.
—Romans 10:9

Make God's Day!
(What can you praise God for today?)

1. _____
2. _____
3. _____
4. _____
5. _____
6. _____
7. _____

Make Someone's Day!
(Be an encourager or a blessing to someone!)

1. _____
2. _____
3. _____
4. _____
5. _____

Make Your Day!
(Create and enjoy memories!)

1. _____
2. _____
3. _____
4. _____
5. _____

(Remember to include names, dates, and places.)

Week 45

My Gratitude Journal

The name of the LORD is a strong tower;
The righteous run to it and are safe.
—Proverbs 18:10

Make God's Day!
(What can you praise God for today?)

1. _____
2. _____
3. _____
4. _____
5. _____
6. _____
7. _____

Make Someone's Day!
(Be an encourager or a blessing to someone!)

1. _____
2. _____
3. _____
4. _____
5. _____

Make Your Day!
(Create and enjoy memories!)

1. _____
2. _____
3. _____
4. _____
5. _____

(Remember to include names, dates, and places.)

Week 46

My Gratitude Journal

For you were bought at a price;
therefore glorify God in your body and in your spirit,
which are God's.
—1 Corinthians 6:20

Make God's Day!
(What can you praise God for today?)

1. _____
2. _____
3. _____
4. _____
5. _____
6. _____
7. _____

Make Someone's Day!
(Be an encourager or a blessing to someone!)

1. _____
2. _____
3. _____
4. _____
5. _____

Make Your Day!
(Create and enjoy memories!)

1. _____
2. _____
3. _____
4. _____
5. _____

(Remember to include names, dates, and places.)

Week 47

My Gratitude Journal

For God has not given us a spirit of fear,
but of power and of love and of a sound mind.
—2 Timothy 1:7

Make God's Day!
(What can you praise God for today?)

1. _____
2. _____
3. _____
4. _____
5. _____
6. _____
7. _____

Make Someone's Day!
(Be an encourager or a blessing to someone!)

1. _____
2. _____
3. _____
4. _____
5. _____

Make Your Day!
(Create and enjoy memories!)

1. _____
2. _____
3. _____
4. _____
5. _____

(Remember to include names, dates, and places.)

Week 48

My Gratitude Journal

Better to be criticized by a wise person
than to be praised by a fool.
—Ecclesiastes 7:5 (NLT)

Make God's Day!
(What can you praise God for today?)

1. _____
2. _____
3. _____
4. _____
5. _____
6. _____
7. _____

Make Someone's Day!
(Be an encourager or a blessing to someone!)

1. _____
2. _____
3. _____
4. _____
5. _____

Make Your Day!
(Create and enjoy memories!)

1. _____
2. _____
3. _____
4. _____
5. _____

(Remember to include names, dates, and places.)

Week 49

My Gratitude Journal

Let the words of my mouth and the meditation of my heart
be acceptable in Your sight,
O LORD, my strength and my Redeemer.
—Psalm 19:14

Make God's Day!
(What can you praise God for today?)

1. _____
2. _____
3. _____
4. _____
5. _____
6. _____
7. _____

Make Someone's Day!
(Be an encourager or a blessing to someone!)

1. _____
2. _____
3. _____
4. _____
5. _____

Make Your Day!
(Create and enjoy memories!)

1. _____
2. _____
3. _____
4. _____
5. _____

(Remember to include names, dates, and places.)

Week 50

My Gratitude Journal

God is faithful, who will not allow you to be tempted
beyond what you are able, but with the temptation
will also make the way of escape, that you may be able to bear it.
—1 Corinthians 10:13b

Make God's Day!
(What can you praise God for today?)

1. _____
2. _____
3. _____
4. _____
5. _____
6. _____
7. _____

Make Someone's Day!
(Be an encourager or a blessing to someone!)

1. _____
2. _____
3. _____
4. _____
5. _____

Make Your Day!
(Create and enjoy memories!)

1. _____
2. _____
3. _____
4. _____
5. _____

(Remember to include names, dates, and places.)

Week 51

My Gratitude Journal

By this all will know that you are My disciples,
if you have love for one another.
—John 13:35

Make God's Day!
(What can you praise God for today?)

1. _____
2. _____
3. _____
4. _____
5. _____
6. _____
7. _____

Make Someone's Day!
(Be an encourager or a blessing to someone!)

1. _____
2. _____
3. _____
4. _____
5. _____

Make Your Day!
(Create and enjoy memories!)

1. _____
2. _____
3. _____
4. _____
5. _____

(Remember to include names, dates, and places.)

Week 52

About the Author

Early on, Carl felt like a *nobody* in a *somebody* world... but later, God changed that perception! The second of seven children, he grew up during the 1940s and '50s in and around Charlotte, North Carolina. In spite of being "poor" by societal standards, he was blessed to be part of a family that valued, cared for, and nurtured each other.

Carl believes his three best decisions in life are:

1. *Accepting Jesus as his personal Savior.* His godly mother taught him well!
2. *Joining the United States Navy.* After leaving high school half-way through his Junior year, he instinctively recognized his need to accept personal responsibility and develop self-discipline.
3. *Marrying Martha.* In retrospect, Carl realized she had been handpicked by God six years before they met! (See Chapter Six).

Carl's business management career began as a communications specialist in the Navy. Following an eight-year career as a Sailor (actually eight years, one month, and 19 days!), he accepted a position with the American Telephone and Telegraph Company (AT&T). Over the next 24 years, he held positions ranging from Communications Technician to District Manager.

Following early retirement from AT&T, Carl founded, developed, and sold a mortgage brokerage company, established a residential lending department for a privately-owned bank, and was Vice President of Operations for a national personnel staffing company.

During and after his business career, Carl's passion has been to help people understand their personal value and the importance of living by godly principles to achieve the best life possible. His desire is that you accept 100% responsibility for your life and *unlock your legacy!*

Carl and Martha live in Loganville, Georgia. Their two children and six grandchildren are scattered hither, thither, and yon!

CPSIA information can be obtained
at www.ICGtesting.com
Printed in the USA
BVHW070157221120
593552BV00004B/6